222 PLAN MANUAL

William L. Owens

Printed by Create Space,
an Amazon.com Company.

Published by
The 222 Plan Ministry

(Training Disciples thru Mentoring)

Originally published in 1973
Eighth Printing

ISBN: 13: 978-1497438514

DEDICATION

I dedicate *The 222 Plan Manual* to Mary Anne who was my faithful marriage partner, and long-suffering friend for forty-eight years. Without her persistent help and encouragement, through editing and proofreading, I would have been unable to complete this writing project.

ACKNOWLEDGMENTS

I am grateful to John Flanagan, Fred King and Chip White. These three friends and fellow servants of Christ have made a considerable sacrifice of their time in editing the eighth revision of the *222 Plan Manual*. Thank you!

I gratefully acknowledge the influence of those whom God has used in my life, many of whom I have not met. However, their ministries were used of God to shape me. Some of my heroes have been the likes of Vance Havner, Francis Schaffer, Steven Olford, Bertha Smith, Lenard Ravenhill, and Norman Grub. I have passed on those gleaned insights in my personal messages, and writings. Often, those insights have become so much a part of my understanding and personality that I have not known where to give proper credit. Therefore, I credit all I know, to God and those whom He has used to teach me.

A few people have been influential in changing the course of my life. It is fitting I honor their contributions:

Harry W. Owens, my father who instilled in me a sense of honesty and an appreciation for law and order in society.

Robert G. Witty, Ph.D. a faithful minister and teacher of the Word who guided me through the challenges of a theological education. He passed to me his high view of Scripture and his discovery of Isaac Watts' method of correlating information in the process of inductive analysis.

Waylon B. Moore, a faithful lover of souls, introduced me to the formal process of discipleship.

My regret is that I have not followed the Lord, nor the influence of these He has given me, to my fullest capacity. I write this manual, not as one who has mastered the process, but as one who is using it as a strategy for living the Christian life.

TABLE OF CONTENTS

HOW TO USE
THE MANUAL

We are introducing a unique plan for training Christians. We call it The 222 Plan. The pilgrimage you are embarking upon is designed to create an opportunity to reach certain goals: (1) a greater degree of spiritual maturity (2) a firm understanding of Bible basics, and (3) a disciplined devotional life of prayer and Bible study.

The *222 Plan Manual* is designed to be used in a one-on-one situation with two believers on a spiritual journey. However, it is possible to make the journey by yourself. Although it is better to travel along with someone for your encouragement and steadfastness, you may make a fruitful journey alone.

Therefore, if you are working through the manual on your own, you will need to find a spiritual counselor. (The counselor can address various Christian life issues as they come up.) Set a date to begin and resolve not to cover more than one session a week. Hold yourself responsible to complete the assignments (including the memory work) before proceeding.

There may also be the possibility that you and another Christian discover the *222 Plan Manual* and desire to make the spiritual journey together. Here, you may take turns leading the weekly sessions. Make sure that each of you consults the mentor's guide after completing your individual session exercises. On occasions, the guide may not satisfy your questions. In such cases, we suggest you consult your pastor or, spiritually mature Bible teacher for clarification.

If you are following a mentor, remember your mentor is not one who has arrived! He or she is a fellow follower after Christ. No one ever graduates from the school of discipleship. It is a lifelong process. You will often be discouraged by your inability to master your life. Don't give up! Remember that every failure is an invitation to succeed. Victory comes through surrender to Christ that will in turn live His life through you.

The "222 Plan" will require a weekly commitment of at least three and one-half hours. The heart of the process is a mentor led work session lasting about an hour. You will need an additional thirty to forty-five minutes per day for four or five days for each week's preparation.

I cannot emphasize enough that the mentor is responsible for checking your progress every week. Be prepared to be held accountable for each works assignments. Accountability is the one essential ingredient in the sessions.

Your ultimate goal is to be available to God so that He may transform you into the likeness of His Son. According to His plan, and by His grace, you will become proficient enough to build these spiritual disciplines into the life of another.

The whole strategy is based on Paul's instruction in II Timothy 2:2. He exhorts Timothy with these words: "And the things that thou hast heard of me among many witnesses, the same commit thou to faithful men, who shall be able to teach others also."

Have a blessed journey and check out our website for other mentoring information at our website: **www. 222plan.org**.

William L. Owens

NOTES

KEYS TO SUCCESSFUL MENTORING

Welcome! If this is your first experience with mentoring, you are commended for committing yourself to making disciples. Our Lord commanded it; therefore, it is an act of obedience and an honorable course of action. We base our particular mentoring strategy on 2 Timothy 2:2. Hence, we call it "The 222 Plan."

There are certain things you need to be aware of regarding this "222 Plan Manual." Note the following:

1.The 222 Plan is designed for one-on-one disciple-making. There are those who maintain that the one-on-one process is too costly regarding time. However, our Lord used it profitably as well as, Paul and Barnabas. While Jesus ministered to the masses, He also invested time in instructing a much smaller group. We see the principle at work when He taught Peter, James, and John. He also taught the entire apostleship numbering twelve. After His resurrection, Jesus mentored Paul in an individual one-on-one session.

2. The Lord is our example. We should teach the masses to identify those who wish to follow Him. Then, single out the faithful or hungry ones for small group and individual sessions where the disciple-maker can transfer his experience and knowledge of Christ's teaching.

3.The goal of the mentor/disciple-maker is to help the disciple to become a reproducer. Therefore, the believer should be committed to sharing with others all he learns in following Christ. Disciple-making has two goals: (1) teaching one to follow Christ by developing spiritual disciplines and (2) teaching him/her to share with someone else to the end that the process is repeated.

4. The Holy Bible is the text. The manual is not "the" essential text for this mentoring process. The Bible is the text, and you should always keep this fact before the disciple. The 222 Plan Manual is a tool to direct the disciple in understanding the basics of the Christian faith. It is a catalyst for discussing the various topics raised in the specific sessions. We measure all discussion by what the Bible says. Our opinion about God and what He teaches must pass the test of agreement with Scripture.

5. Completion of the manual is not the end! The completion of these twenty-six sessions is not the end, but rather the entrance into a lifelong process of ever growing in the grace of our Lord Jesus Christ.

6. The goal is building disciplined disciples of Christ. You should view the manual as an ally in building the necessary disciplines into the disciple's life. Therefore, don't hesitate to supplement the materials in the manual with whatever is helpful in your own Christian experience. It may help your disciple too.

7. Keep the disciple challenged! Remember, these materials are basic! You should challenge the disciple's ability. Keep the person you are leading mentally stretched. If the assignments are too easy add supplementary assignments or the disciple may lose interest. For example, if you are dealing with a person who has much Biblical knowledge, seek a fuller explanation of the answers when reviewing the material.

8. You too are a learner! Don't try to give the impression that you have mastered all the information or disciplines. No one but Christ has ever done so. Therefore, work at conveying the idea that you are a leader that is also being mentored.

9. Do not mentor the opposite sex.
Avoid all potentially dangerous circumstances. Even if the parties are above any suspicion, there is still an issue of the possible appearance of evil. (The exception would be when agreeing to disciple a married couple.)

Keep the above points in view as you make this journey into the experience of disciple-making. Don't be intimated by your inexperience. As one mentoring friend said: "Any committed Christian can mentor another—all he has to do is stay one step ahead."

Don't worry about not having all the answers. The best trained pastors are often stymied by the childlike questions of zealous minds. Learn to say, "I don't know, but I'll try to find out." You are not expected to know everything! (If you are a pastor or other formally trained person, you, also need to observe the above principle.)

The best thing you can do is to find a spiritual confidant with whom you can share the joys and pains of the mentoring process. Seek help from those you know to have spiritual wisdom. Ask them to help you when seeking answers to the disciple's questions. Generally, the answers you seek will be more spiritual in nature than academic.

Be transparent in your relationship with the disciple. Let your humanity show!

HOW TO CONDUCT THE ACCOUNTABILITY SESSION
(Instruction for Mentors)

You need to meet with the disciple at least once each week. Our goal for these sessions is to assist the learner in his spiritual journey. Treat seriously the time being spent. We divide the accountability sessions into distinct segments, and each is designed to build spiritual character in the mentoring process.

Choose your meeting place carefully. It is best to meet on neutral ground, but avoid the church if possible. Over the years, I have used the fast-food restaurant with great advantage. It may be noisy and crowded, but it is amazing how little attention people pay you. I have breakfast with my fellow learner, and then we review the previous week's assignment in the following order:

Bible Study— We discuss first any problems he may have had in answering the assigned questions. Then, the questions are used to launch a discussion in an area that you perceive the learner is weak or needs better understanding. If the disciple is a new Christian, then cover the questions point-by-point. With the more mature Christian, you need only talk about the areas that might have given him trouble.

Scripture Memory Review— Almost every week there will be an assigned Scripture for memorization. Admittedly, a few weeks are scheduled as review. Reinforce the exercise of memorizing Scripture. If one wants the Word hidden in their heart, then Scripture memorization is essential. Refer to the assignments at the beginning of each session's lesson and ask that the disciples cite the applicable Scripture word-for-word. The keys to successful Scripture memorization are steadfastness and review.

Daily Devotion Time— Check for evidence that your partner is meeting with God daily. Tell him or her to anticipate keeping a spiritual journal. The importance of recording spiritual thoughts will be introduced during the mentoring process. (The sample journal form at the end of the lesson may be reproduced.)

Sermon Outlines— From the start, expect the disciple to take notes on messages delivered where he or she worships weekly. Ask to see the outline at each of your sessions. Ask the following questions: "Were you aware of God speaking with you?" and "What are you planning to do about it?" You may wish to ask other questions. Be sensitive to the needs of the disciple and remember your goal—to make him or her spiritually successful. Do not give the impression that taking notes is busy work. Note-taking is a process designed to increase one's ability to concentrate on content and to listen to God's voice for proper action. (A sample sermon note form is supplied and may be reproduced if desired.)

Supplemental Material & Assignments— At the end of some of the study questions, there are materials that relate to the subject or to a discipline being introduced at that point in the process. If such is applicable, then you should discuss it with the disciple at your weekly session. Your goal is to communicate concepts. Continue to discuss the matter until you are certain the disciple has an adequate handle on the issue at hand.

Prayer— Before closing the weekly accountability session you should have a time of prayer. If you are meeting in a public place, pause and retire to a place of privacy. I usually invite my friend to join me in my car for this intimate time with God. The prayer time is primarily for adoration and intercession. You will want to teach by example. Begin by taking the lead. Ask, "Do you have a specific prayer need?"

Follow these guidelines: 1. As you pray—be yourself 2. Focus on God—give Him praise before presenting petitions. 3. Avoid the temptation to impress the disciple. 4. Talk to God—not to the other party present.

After the third or fourth session, invite the disciple to take a more active part in the prayer time. Ask him to join you in petitioning the Lord. Have the disciple to pray first? Listen carefully and discern needs your partner may have, then when it's your turn, intercede for him as you bring the prayer session to a close.

Watch for things that need to be dealt with during seasons of prayer. However, never correct your brother's prayer unless there is gross error. Conduct constructive criticism in a spirit of humility. If in prayer, you become aware of an unbiblical request or lack of understanding, make a note of it and deal with it in the next meeting or when the subject is about a future session. At all costs, avoid condemning the prayer of another.

Weekly Assignment— Before parting, make sure you have a clear understanding about expectations for the next session. Go over each item on the lesson sheet regarding the next week's assignment. Be sure you have a meeting of the minds about what is expected. (Make obvious use of the personal pronoun "we." Use "we" because you want the disciple to know you are submitting yourself to the same disciplines you are asking of him.)

Be sure to leave with an encouraging word.

222: THE MASTER'S PLAN SESSION 1

THE GOD OF THE BIBLE

Assignment for Session 1:
    a. Complete: Questions for *God of the Bible*
    b. Memorize: Deuteronomy 6:4
    c. Conduct: Daily Devotions

Introductory Summary: God reveals Himself through the Bible and creation. The following Scriptures will reveal some facts about God that will aid you in spiritual growth. Use your own words in answering the questions, unless, you are asked to fill in blanks with a key word from Scripture. Questions are intended to promote conceptual understanding. Therefore, try to find meaning in the context of the passages studied—not just the verse referenced.

Questions:

1. God has a plan for believers. How does Ephesians 4:1show this fact?

2. Three characteristics of personality are intelligence, emotion and volition. Correspondingly, God thinks, feels, and acts. What emotion does God show in John 3:16?

Note: God is not a "force" for good; He is a personal non-created being. He is self-sustaining. When Moses asked God who should he say sent him to be Israel's leader, God's response was— tell Israel "I Am" sends you. In this name "I Am" rests the eternal nature of God. He is consistently present in the present tense. He has no past. He has no future for He is eternal.

3.   What are we taught from Deuteronomy 6:4? (Genesis1:26,11:7)

4.   Is there a Biblical basis for believing there is a plural personality in the God-head? State how each of the following verses illustrates God's plurality in a singular Godhead.

    a. Luke 4:18

    b. John 3:5

    c. Romans 8:11

    d. Ephesians 2:18

    e. Hebrews 9:14

5. How do the following verses show the fact of Christ's deity?

a. Matthew 9:2-7

b. Matthew 28:20

c. John 1:1-3

d. John 17:5, 26

6. There is a third person in the Godhead who is equally God with the first and second Persons. How do the following verses show the Trinity in the Godhead?

a. Luke 12:10,12

b. John 16:7-14

c. II Peter 1:21

NOTES

Mentor's Guide—Lesson 1
The God of the Bible

The number to the left corresponds to the question number on the Lesson one question sheet.

1. The believer was chosen by God to be holy. Therefore, the believer exists to reflect the holiness of God in his life.

2. God's ability to act with compassion reveals His capacity for love, which is part of His personality.

3. Deuteronomy 6:4 teaches us that God is one God. He is one in number, but He is a plurality. He is the God of unity.

4. Each verse emphasizes a different member of the God head as the central actor but with the other members being involved.
   a. Luke 4:18 Christ is speaking; the Spirit is anointing Him and He (the Son) acknowledges that the Father has sent Him on mission.
   b. John 3:5 Here we have the Son speaking, the Spirit is referenced as the One who births people into the Father's kingdom.
   c. In Romans 8:11 The Spirit of the Father is seen as having raised the Son from the dead by the power of the Holy Spirit.
   d. Ephesians 2:18 shows us that we have access to the Father, through the Son, in the power of the Spirit.

e. Hebrews. 9:14 All three of the persons of the Godhead are here referenced: Christ's blood through the eternal Spirit the living God (Father).

5. Christ's divinity is proclaimed in the Scriptures. The following examples illustrate His divinity by revealing:
   a. His power to heal and to forgive sins (Matthew 9:2-7).
   b. His ability to be present with them at all times (Matthew 28:20).
   c. His power to create (John 1:1-3).
   d. His presence with the Father before the world was created (John 17:5,26).

6. The Holy Spirit's reality is shown in the following Verses by:
   a. It being an unforgivable sin to speak against Him (Luke 12:10)
   b. His work in the world—convicting the world of sin, of righteousness, and of judgment to come (John 16:7-14).
   c. His moving upon chosen men to write the Scriptures (II Peter 1:21).

WEEKLY DISCIPLINES: Make assignments in accordance with the weekly assignment sheet.

222: THE MASTER'S PLAN
SESSION 2

GOD AND CREATION

Assignment for Session 2:
  a. Complete: Questions for *God and Creation*
  b. Memorize: Colossians 1:16, 17
  c. Conduct: Daily Devotions
  d. Take: Sermon notes

Introductory Summary: The Biblical teaching about the one God that demonstrates plurality in unity must now be enlarged. Two dimensions need to be added: (1) His created work and (2) His work in His created world.

This Bible study is to give emphasis to His work in creation. One essential characteristic must be appreciated when considering creation: God is sovereign. Only His "will" limits or determines His work. Study the Bible's testimony about the act and nature of creation.

Questions:

1. Compare Ephesians 1:11 and Revelation 4:11. State your conclusions in your own words. Focus your remarks on the will of God in relation to His act of creation.

2. Read and meditate upon Colossians 1:16, 17. What insight do you gain about God prior to creation?

3. Using Psalm 33:9 as your authority, list the ingredients God used to create the world.

4. How did He create? (Psalm 33:9)

5. What did God create? (Genesis 1:1)

6. Nehemiah 9:6 declares the fact that God created the
_____.

Note: The Lord not only created the material universe but angels and man as well. He made them as created beings. They are not an extension of Himself or a part of Himself. All created beings are separate entities from God.

7. God expressed His attitude about His creation work in Genesis 1:31. Discuss what this means to you.

8. Creation is the act of causing what did not exist to come into being. The following verses describe some characteristic of God's person in creation. (Use one to four words for each reference.)

Romans 1:20

Isaiah 40:26, 28

Psalm19:1

Psalm 33:6

Psalm 104:24

Revelation 4:1

NOTES

MENTOR'S GUIDE - LESSON 2
GOD AND CREATION

Your goal in this lesson is to assist the disciple in understanding the Biblical account of creation. The author takes a literal interpretation of the Bible. We hope to persuade others to take the same view but will be tolerant of other views as long as Christ is acknowledged as God's only begotten Son—there is no salvation in any other. (I hope you share the author's view. If you do not, then I would suggest that you settle that issue with God before proceeding with the mentoring process.) We cannot force our convictions upon others. Remember this little ditty "If you convince a man, against his will, he is of the same opinion still."

Therefore, lead the disciple to seek God's mind for only then will one feel confident of the chosen position. Always come back to the question, "What says the Word of God?" If God's Word (the Holy Bible) is not the final authority for our belief system, then we are left with only one option—a sea of human opinions.

Avoid expressions of human opinion at the expense of God's revealed Truth. "Let God be true and every man a liar."

1. Look for an appreciation of God's sovereignty in all matters. If the disciple's answer does not reveal a proper acknowledgment of God's sovereignty, then lead him to focus on the word "will" in each verse.

2.   Lead the disciple to see that God has always existed. He is the great "I Am." While you may take His self-existence for granted, people often fail to give it a second thought. God had no creator! Lead the disciple to accept this fact by faith.

3.   According to Psalm 33:9, the two key words or elements in creation are "spoke" and "commanded."

4.   According to Psalm 33:9, God exercised His will and spoke the world into existence. (Lead the disciple to affirm that God has power without limit.)

5.   According to Genesis 1:1, God created the heavens and the earth. (It is to be understood that the word "heavens" refers to all that exists outside of the atmosphere of "Earth.")

6.   The blank should be filled in with "heaven" or "heavens."
(Note: God created the angelic beings. You may choose to talk about the differences in the material and the im material worlds. Be warned! Do not let your speculations lead you into error.)

7.   The disciple should have an answer that emphasizes God's pleasure with His creation. Take this opportunity to talk about the meaning of creation and the things it implies about God and man. Just make sure your conclusions are biblical.

8. The responses you are to expect from this question are as follows:

Romans 1:20	God's eternal power
Isaiah 40:26, 28	Everlasting God
Psalm19:1	The glory of God
Psalm 33:6	The Word of the Lord
Psalm 104:24	The wisdom of God
Revelation 4:1	Created for His pleasure

Don't be too strict in applying these answers—allow tolerance. However, take care to point out the above characteristics.

WEEKLY DISCIPLINES: Continue all weekly disciplines. Follow the assignment sheet closely. Make sure you check memory verses, sermon notes, etc.

NOTES

222: THE MASTER'S PLAN SESSION 3

GOD AND MAN

Assignment for Session 3
    a. Complete: Questions for *God and Man*
    b. Memorize: Romans 5:12
    c. Conduct: Daily Devotions
    d. Take: Sermon Notes
    e. Study: the "Word Chart" on page 37

Introductory Summary: God did not make us to abandon us. He is benevolently interested in our welfare and our relationship to Him. Our study will focus on man's personal relationship with God.

Questions:

1. According to Genesis 2:7, God made man from the _____ of the ground.

2. Genesis 1:26 declares that God made us in His image. (Discuss what this means.)

3. Discuss Genesis 2:16-17. (Ask your mentor to explain the meaning of death.)

4. Genesis 3:1-20 describes the account of Adam and Eve's sin. Was this willful sin? Explain!

5. How does Genesis 3:7 show Adam and Eve's feeling of guilt?

6. Based on the authority of Genesis 3:17, 18, "How much of God's creation was affected by sin?" Explain your answer!

7. Look up each of the following references and record their basic message:

Romans 5:12,17

Isaiah 53:6

Romans 3:10-12, 23

Galatians 3:10

8. When is man under God's judgment? (John 3:18, 36)

NOTES

FIVE WAYS TO GET THE WORD INTO YOUR LIFE

I
HEAR THE WORD
(ROMANS 10:17)

II
READ THE WORD
(REVELATION 1:3)

III
STUDY THE WORD
(ACTS 17:11)

IV
MEMORIZE THE WORD
(PSALM 119:9, 11)

V
MEDITATE ON THE WORD
(PSALM 1:2, 3)

NOTES

Mentor's Guide—Session 3
God and Man

Knowing the reality of how God and man relate is essential to a person's spiritual growth. Lead the disciple to accept by faith the statements of Scripture. However, note the difference between blind faith and reasoned faith. God does not ask us to trust Him blindly. This truth is one of the essential differences between Christianity and the world's religions.

God did not make man to abandon him. Our loving Father has taken great care that we understand His desire. God has chosen that His people please Him by believing what He says. Believing what God says is to have faith in God. Such faith is not a leap in the dark. It is a steadfast focus of the heart on believing the specific Word of God. When God told Abraham to leave the land of Ur, He gave Abraham a definite word—specific instructions. He knew that it was God that had spoken and that God was trustworthy.

Take great care to impress the disciple with an awareness of God's desire to have a love relationship with him. You also may be struggling to gain a realization of His love. The key is to trust and obey! God is at work in our world and is impacting it through His unique relationship with His children. A lasting effect on life requires an abiding sense of divine love.

Therefore, seek to maintain this reality in your own life and teach the disciple to do the same.

1. The key word is "dust." Dust is the element God mentions as man's key physical ingredient.

2. The concept of being made in the image of God may have several implications. My personal conviction is that the best way to interpret this phrase is to assume that man is like God in every aspect of his being. For example, as God is three parts and yet one, man is also three parts yet one. God is Father, Son, and Spirit. A man is body, soul, and spirit. (The subject will be dealt with more thoroughly in another session.)

3. Death has two applications, physical and spiritual. Physical death is the cessation of animated life. Spiritual death is eternal separation from God. Both forms of death come to mankind as the result of personal sin. Because we inherit the sin nature from Adam, we are classified as sinners before we commit sin. We do not become sinners by sinning, But, rather, we sin because we are sinners. Therefore, we are spiritually dead and require Christ's redemption. Coming in faith to Christ will provide us spiritual life. However, being sinners, all men face physical death. But, those who refuse the witness of God's Spirit about Christ will experience spiritual death which is separation from God in eternity.

4. Adam and Eve willfully sinned. One may judge them guilty of willful sin because they clearly understood the command of God and rebelled anyway.

5. Guilt is shown through their knowledge of nakedness.

Prior to partaking of the forbidden fruit, both Adam and Eve were untroubled by their naked state (Gen. 2:25). However, having eaten from the tree of the knowledge of good and evil, they became ashamed of their nakedness because they had lost their innocence.

6. The text clearly states that our human parents and the earth on which they lived were cursed because of their willful disobedience. Because of their sin God exercised perfect judgment and therefore everything in the universe moves toward decay and not restoration. God's ultimate goal is the restoration of all things including His glory and the salvation of mankind. Jesus, in His high priestly prayer, prayed for the restoration of His glory. (John 17) (Discourage discussion beyond the lesson's focus. However, try to satisfy pertinent questions.)

7. The following passages teach something of man's current spiritual state:

Romans 5:12,17 show that sin has reigned over man since the sin of Adam and Eve in the garden.

Isaiah 53:6 has reference to Man's inward inclination toward self-serving which is sin and became part of man's nature after Adam sinned.

Romans 3:10-12, 23 According to these verses, no natural son of Adam has a desire to live for God. His sinful state necessitates God providing a means of salvation. He offers His only Son as a sacrifice for the sins of those who will trust Him.

Galatians 3:10 teaches us not to depend on keeping the Law for God's approval. We cannot keep God's standard before being "born again." While a believer strives to live by the Law, he does not depend on his keeping it to gain favor with God. He knows that only the blood of God's own Son will satisfy God's righteous demands.

8. A person is under the judgment of God's wrath when there is a lack of trust or personal dependence upon the finshed work of Christ on that person's behalf.

SUPPLEMENTARY MATERIAL
Study and explain *Five Ways To Get The Word Into Your Life*. Be prepared to talk about the significance of these five ways of getting the Word of God into ones life. (Ensure that the disciple understands that he is responsible for explaining the chart at session three.)

KEY: Clarify the differences between "study" and "meditate." The exercise of studying is the pursuit of knowledge while meditation is a devotional act of reflection. In our case, we are seeking knowledge of revealed Truth. Then, we reflect devotionally on that Truth until we have an understanding we can apply to daily living.

Record your insight below as you study the chart.

222: THE MASTOR'S PLAN SESSION 4

SALVATION AND CHRIST

Assignment for Session 4
    a. Complete: Questions for *Salvation and Christ*
    b. Memorize: John 3:16
    c. Conduct: Daily Devotions
    d. Take: Sermon Notes

Introductory Summary: There are several interpretations of how man can be reconciled to God. It appears that these philosophies of salvation ultimately fall into one of two categories: the first suggests that God has created access to salvation through Christ and the rest is up to man; the second proclaims that all that can be done for man has been completed in Christ's death and resurrection and all that is necessary is the exercising of 'faith' in Christ and receive God's salvation gift by 'grace.' Let's see what the Bible says!

Questions:

1. Sinners have earned the wages of _____. (Romans 6:23) Are these wages physical or spiritual? Why have you given this answer?

2. God does not want to render to us our wages. He wishes to grant us a gift. According to John 3:15-16 who may receive the gift of God?

3. What is the work of God revealed in John 6:29? Explain your answer.

4. On what basis is mankind under the sentence of eternal separation from God? Reference: Romans 5:12. What does this mean?

5. In Genesis 3:15, 21, how do these verses convey God's promise of a coming Savior?

6. Read Genesis 4:3-17 and discuss the worship of Cain and Abel. (Why was Cain's worship not acceptable?)

7. Read Genesis 22:1-18. In this passage, verse fourteen ties the events of this chapter into the coming death of Christ two thousand years later. Compare verse two with II Chronicles 3:1. Discuss how this passage illustrates the Messiah and His death as a substitute for man's sin.

8. How were Abraham and David saved? (Romans 4:1-8) Explain how you know your answer is true.

9. When we, by faith, receive Christ as Lord, we receive the same spiritual blessing that _____ received. (Galatians 3:13, 14) Explain the meaning of your answer.

10. A Holy God cannot excuse sin! God's holiness prevents Him from excusing sin. With the previous statement in mind, read Philippians 2:7, 8. On what basis can God forgive Sin?

Note: Salvation is provided by faith in what God promises. This truth is shown in Hebrews 11 in which one may readily ascertain that we please God on the same basis as Old Testament saints.

MENTOR'S GUIDE— SESSION 4
SALVATION AND CHRIST

Session four is critical to the disciple-making process. If the disciple is merely a professor of Christ and not a possessor, then this session will most likely reveal his condition. Therefore, be sensitive to the disciple's spirit as he shares in this session.

1. The Key correct words are "sin" and "spiritual." These are the true, because sin is committed in the heart before one actually commits the act.

2. The one who "believes" on Him receives the gift of eternal life. This belief is not just believing facts about His identity and what He's done. Biblical faith is a working belief that produces action. James says faith without works is "dead." (James 2:17)

3. The work of God is the exercising of faith in Him. The work God wants from those who serve Him is action based on trust—trust in who He is and what He has been and is doing.

4. Mankind is under the judgment of God's wrath because of unbelief. Man does not believe on the name of God's Son. Therefore, he is lost and separated from God. It is not because of how one behaves that he is approved but how he believes. (However you must be sure your disciple understands that what one believes determines how one behaves.)

5. It would be difficult to see a Messianic promise from this passage, if we did not have the advantage of the New Testament's teaching about salvation and the necessity for the shedding of blood. However, because of Hebrews 9:22 that says: ". . .without the shedding of blood there is no remission of sin," we have a key to understanding these verses.

In verse fifteen of our question text, we have a prophecy that conveys to us the sacrifice of Christ for the sin of the world. Satan is seen here as a temporary victor who will be vanquished. In verse twenty-one God illustrated the importance of the blood sacrifice when He provided the covering of animal skins for Adam and Eve. There is no direct statement about how the skins were made available; it is reasonable to assume that God sacrificed the lives of the animals. He later instituted the system of blood sacrifice to illustrate the ultimate sacrifice of His only begotten Son for the sins of the world.

6. Cain and Abel illustrate the two types of people who worship God. Cain is like people who devise their "own ways" of worship, while Abel represents people who follow God instruction for worship.

7. The present question has to do with God as a covenant keeper. God had promised Abraham that through Isaac he would be the father of a large nation. If Isaac were sacrificed, how could the promise be fulfilled?

(In verse 14 of Genesis 22, God reveals the provision of a living sacrifice. It is significant that He named the place "God Will Provide." Verse two of the text and 2 Chronicles 3:1 are tied together by showing that David is a product of

God's promise to Abraham. (While God spared Abraham's son, He didn't spare His own! Why? Because, without the shedding of blood there is no remission of sin.)

8. Abraham and David were saved. They were saved the same way all people in all generations must be saved. They trusted what God said and acted on the Truth. True faith in God takes action because of what is believed. While we are not saved by our doing, the saved will do what God says because they love Him and want to honor Him.

9. "Abraham," is the supplied word. Therefore, all who now trust in Christ are recipients of the same spiritual blessing promised to Abraham.

10. God will forgive sin only when the sin has been paid for by one who is acceptable to Him. God forgives sin, but He cannot forgive unless His perfect law has been satisfied. Christ, being without sin, was qualified as a sacrifice for payment for the sins of the world. The Father is now free to forgive all who will rely on the work of His Son as atonement for their sin.

(God cannot excuse sin! To excuse something is to pretend that the thing did not happen. God must maintain His integrity. Therefore, He cannot excuse but He can forgive. Forgiveness may only be offered when a person meets the qualifications. True faith in God will lead to repentance and confession of sin. God's justice and His law are satisfied through His Son. His mercy is freely given. True faith in God will lead to repentance and confession. God's justice, and His law are satisfied through the obedience of His Son.

His mercy is freely given to all who will abandon themselves to Christ.)

MEMORY VERSE
Today's assigned memory verse is Ephesians 2:8, 9. I have two principles that apply to this vital activity.

First, I will encourage and coach the disciple until he either memorizes the passage or becomes so frustrated that memorization is impossible.

Second, if apparently the disciple cannot memorize the verse, then I hold him accountable for the location (e.g. Ephesians 2:8, 9).

He must also provide a conceptual analysis of each verse. Don't allow a disciple to continue this process if he shows no understanding of the Truth. Because he must teach and model these principles before others, he must have a firm grasp of the Biblical content.

DEVOTIONS
The disciple should give evidence of having communed daily with the Lord through Bible reading and prayer. Look for this evidence and challenge him if you perceive he is not maintaining a personal devotional life. One way you can motivate him is to show him one of your completed spiritual journal sheets. Duplicate the sample sheet found at the back of the workbook for repeated use. Show him how you use it and then tell him you expect to see something similar when you meet for the next session.

SERMON NOTES

One of the essential ingredients in the disciple's training is the sensitizing of his mind to analyze and organize what he reads and hears. Therefore, we must learn to capitalize on every opportunity to build our knowledge base. Share with your disciple how note taking can help build a base of information for use in our own lives and in the mentoring of another. (Introduce the Listening or Reading Sheet. Show how to use it by filling one out in his presence. You may freely duplicate this sheet or use it for instance to design your own.)

NOTES

222: THE MASTOR'S PLAN SESSION 5

ASSURANCE OF SALVATION

Assignment for Session 5
    a. Complete: Questions for *Assurance of Salvation*
    b. Memorize: John 5:24
    c. Conduct: Daily Devotions
    d. Take: Sermon Notes
    e. Study: the "Importance of Devotions" on page 57
    f. Begin: "Spiritual Journal" page 63, 64

Introductory Summary: You have come to know Christ as Savior. You began by repenting of your sins, placing your faith in Him, and asking for his forgiveness.
Now, you show your dependance on Christ and His Spirit to lead you into a life of faithfulness. Your life is in Him (I John 5:11) and you have given yourself to Him. Now, that you know Him, you want your daily activities to show that you love Christ. Our purpose is to show that God gives assurance to all who trust and obeys Him (I John 1:7).

Questions:

1. Look up the following Scripture references and record the promise God gives.

    a. John 10:28

    b. Hebrews 10:16, 17

    c. John 5:24

    d. John 14: 2, 3

    e. I Peter 1:3-5

    f. Hebrews 4:9

    g. II Timothy 4:8

    h. I Peter 5:4

    i. John 14:26

    j. John 16:13

    k. Acts 1:8

    l. II Corinthians 3:16

2. In Numbers 23:19, God commits Himself to those who have faith in Him. What is the commitment He makes?

3. Read I John 5:13. Record below, what God promises believers.

4. From Romans 8:16, explain how God's Spirit works with your spirit to help you know you are one of His children. Consult Galatians 4:6 and I John 4:1.

5. Read Romans 8:35-39 and fill in the blank. _____ can separate you from the love of God, which is in Christ Jesus.

6. Read John 6:39; Luke 21:18; John 10:28, 29. Record the central theme of these verses.

7. In Galatians 3:26 God says that you are one of His children because you have _____ in Jesus.

8. Study Hebrews 2:11; Matthew 12:50; and Luke 8:21. Record your thoughts about the central theme of these verses as it relates to the believer.

9. At this moment, what is Christ doing for believers? Read Romans 8:34; Hebrews 7:25; and Hebrews 8:1, then record your answer below.

10. God says that people will know that you are one of His disciples by one particular trait. Read John 13:35; John 15:12; and James 2:5 and discuss this trait.

THE IMPORTANCE
OF DEVOTIONS

By: The Reverend George Muller

It has pleased the Lord to teach me a truth, the benefit of which I have not lost for more than fourteen years. The point is this: I saw more clearly than ever that the first great and primary business to which I ought to attend every day was to have my soul happy in the Lord. The first thing to be concerned about was not how much I might serve the Lord, or how I might glorify the Lord; but how I might get my soul into a happy state and how my inner man might be nourished. For I might seek to set the truth before the un-converted, I might seek to benefit believers, I might seek to relieve distresses, I might in other ways seek to behave myself as it becomes a child of God in this world; and yet, not being happy in the Lord, and not being nourished and strengthened in my inner man day by day, all this might not be attended to in a right spirit. Before this time my practice had been, at least for ten years previously, as a habitual thing, to give myself to prayer after having dressed myself in the morning.

Now I give myself to the reading of the Word of God, and to meditate on it, that thus my heart might be comforted, encouraged, warned, reproved, instructed; and that thus, by means of the Word of God whilst meditating on it, my heart be brought into experimental communion with the Lord. I began, therefore, to meditate on the New Testament, from the beginning, early in the morning. The first thing I did, after having asked in a few words of the Lord's blessing upon His precious Word, was to begin to meditate on the Word of God, searching, as it were, into every verse to get blessing out of it; not for the sake of the public ministry of the Word, not for the sake of preaching on what I meditated upon, but for the sake of obtaining food for my own soul. The result I have found to be almost invariably this, that after a very few minutes my soul has been led to confession, or to thanksgiving, or to intercession, or to supplication; so that, though I did not, as it were, give myself to prayer, but to meditation, yet it turned almost immediately, more or less, into prayer.

When, thus, I have been for a while making confession or intercession or supplication or have given thanks, I go on to the next words or verse, turning all, as I go into prayer for myself or others, as the Word may lead to it, but still continually keeping before me that food for my own souls in the object of my meditation. The result of this is that there is always a good deal of confession, thanksgiving, supplication, or intercession mingled with my meditation, and that my inner man almost invariably is even sensibly nourished and strengthened, and that by breakfast time, with rare exceptions, I am in a peaceful if not happy state of heart. Thus, also, the Lord is pleased to communicate unto me that which, either very soon after or at a later time, I have found to become food for other believers, though it was not for the sake of the public ministry of the Word that I gave myself to meditation, but for the profit of my own inner man.

With this mode I have likewise combined the being out in the open air for an hour, and hour and a half, or two hours, before breakfast, walking about in the fields, and in the summer sitting for a little on the stiles, if I find it too much to walk all the time. I find it very beneficial to my health to walk thus for meditation before breakfast, and am now so in the habit of using the time for that purpose, that when I get into the open air I generally take out a New Testament of good size type, which I carry with me for that purpose, besides my Bible; and I find that I can profitably spend my time in the open air, which formerly was not the case for want of habit. I used to consider the time spent in walking a loss, but now I find it very profitable, not only to my body, but also to my soul. The walking out before breakfast is, of course, not necessarily connected with this matter, and everyone has to judge according to his strength and other circumstances.

The difference, then, between my former practice and my present one is this; formerly, when I rose, I began to pray as soon as possible, and generally spent all my time till breakfast in prayer, or almost all the time. At all events I almost invariably began with prayer, except when I felt my soul to be more than usually barren; in which case I read the Word of God for food, or for refreshment, or for revival and renewal of my inner man, before I gave myself to prayer. But what was the result? I often spent a quarter of an hour, or half hour, or even one hour, on my knees, before being conscious to myself of having derived comfort, encouragement, humbling of soul, etc.

Often after having suffered much from wandering of mind for the first ten minutes, or quarter of an hour, or even half an hour, I only then began really to pray. I scarcely ever suffer now in this way. For my heart being nourished by the Truth, being brought into experimental fellowship with

God, I speak to my Father and to my Friend (vile though I am, and unworthy of it) about the things that He has brought before me in His precious Word.

It often now astonishes me that I did not sooner see this point. In no book did I ever read about it. No public ministry ever brought the matter before me. No private intercourse with a brother stirred me up to this matter. And, yet now, since God has taught me this point, it is as plain to me as anything, that the first thing the child of God has to do, morning by morning, is to obtain food for his inner man. As the outward man is not fit for work for any length of time except we take food, and as this is one of the first things we do in the morning, so it should be with the inner man. We should take food for that, as everyone must allow. Now, what is the food for the inner man? Not prayer, but the Word of God, so that it only passes through our minds, just as water runs through a pipe but considering what we read, pondering over it, and applying it to our hearts.

When we pray, we speak to God. Now prayer, in order to be continued for any length of time in any other than a formal manner requires, generally speaking, a measure of strength or godly desire, and the season, therefore, when this exercise of the soul can be most effectively performed is after the inner man has been nourished by meditation on the Word of God, where we find our Father speaking to us, to encourage us, to comfort us, to instruct us, to humble us, to reprove us. We may, therefore, profitably meditate, with God's blessing, though we are ever so weak spiritually; nay, the weaker we are, the more we need meditation for the strengthening of our inner man. Thus there is far less to be feared from wandering of mind than if we give ourselves to prayer without having had time previously for meditation.

I dwell so particularly on this point because of the immense spiritual profit and refreshment I am conscious of having derived from it myself, and I affectionately and solemnly beseech all my fellow believers to ponder this matter. By the blessing of God, I ascribe to this mode the help and strength which I have had from God to pass in peace through deeper trials, in various ways, than I had ever had before; and after having now about fourteen years tried this way, I can most fully, in the fear of God, commend it.
In addition to this, I generally read, after family prayer, larger Word of God, when I still pursue my practice of reading regularly onward in the Holy Scriptures, sometimes in the New Testament and sometimes in the Old, and for more than twenty-six years, I have proved the blessedness of it. I take also, either then or at other parts of the day, time more especially for prayer.

How different, when the soul is refreshed and made happy early in the morning, from what it is when, without spiritual preparation, the service, the trials, and the temptations of the day come upon me.

May 9th, 1841 (From *Autobiography of George Muller*, p. 152)

NOTES

222 PLAN: SPIRITUAL JOURNAL

DATE	ENTRY

222 PLAN: SPIRITUAL JOURNAL

DATE	ENTRY

Mentor's Guide— Session 5
Assurance of Salvation

You will notice that each session will build on the previous session. Therefore, it is important that you discern a high level of comprehension and spiritual understanding in the disciple before proceeding.

We now take up a subject with which many Christians wrestle. Many are too ashamed to confess their struggle lest they appear to have an inferior faith. Only God knows when a person has genuinely been "born again." While you may have a "witness of the Spirit" about someone's salvation, you must be careful, because the experience is subjective in nature and one may make an error in discernment. It is not the mentor's responsibility to talk a person into believing his soul is in a state of grace. The Spirit of God is the only one who can truly convince a person regarding spiritual safety. The mentor's job is one of encouragement. You encourage him as he grows in grace and rebuke him when you become aware of sin creeping into his life. It is easier to talk about rebuke than to carry it out. Just remember, all correction must be motivated by a loving desire to see him succeed.

In this session, you will teach the disciple that assurance of one's spiritual relationship to God is found in the Word of God. No other source will provide adequate assurance and peace to the believer's soul. Lead the Christian to refuse to trust his own feelings. Teach him to be objective in his dealings with spiritual things. Experiences are precious, but we often depend on them to the neglect of what the Bible teaches. Don't let that happen to you! Teach the disciple not to place too much confidence in experiences. Ultimately, we can only trust what God teaches. (Do not interpret these words as being an attack on a genuine "new birth" experience. If one does not experience the "new birth," there is no Biblical salvation.)

1. Note the promises made by the Scriptures below:
    a. John 10:28: God promises eternal life to believers and also promises them security for none will be snatched from His hand.

    b. Hebrews 1:16-17: He will put His laws in the heart and mind; he will not remember their sins against them.

    c. John 5:24: He will grant everlasting life to those who believe the testimony of Christ.

    d. John 14:2-3: He promises us that a place is being prepared for us and that Christ will return to receive us to Himself.

    e. I Peter 1:3-5: He promises to reserve for us a crown of incorruptible inheritance in heaven.

    f. Hebrews 4:9: God promises us a supernatural rest.

    g. II Timothy 4:8: God has laid up a righteous crown for those who love His appearing.

    h. I Peter 5:4: He promises the believer a crown of glory that will not fade.

i.   John 14:26: He promised to send the Holy Spirit in His absence.

j.   John 16:13: He promises the Holy Spirit will guide us into all Truth.

k.   Acts 1:8: He promised—His disciples—the Holy Spirit would come upon them in power and He would make them fishers of men.

l.   II Corinthians 3:16: He promises to remove the veil that hides spiritual Truth from us.

2.   In Numbers 23:19 God has assured the reader that He can be counted upon to keep His word. Whatever God says, He will do it.

3.   I John 5:13 affirms that God wants His children to know they possess eternal life.

4.   The Holy Spirit actually gives the believer assurance by bearing a personal witness in the heart. How the Spirit bears the witness is not clear, but the fact that He does is undeniable. The reality of His witness based on Scripture is the final authority for confidence.

5.   The Romans eight passage is presented as assurance that nothing can separate the child of God from the Lord. (Reason with the disciple. Make sure he understands the analogy of birth. No one can undo one's own physical birth, also the spiritual birth is permanent.)

6. The three references in question number six offer believers a sense of tremendous security as children of God.

7. The blank should be filled with the word "faith."

8. Lead the disciple to see that each believer is united with Christ. (Stress that this unity is more than a mere theory. Our unity with Christ is an accomplished fact and a spiritual reality.)

9. Christ's primary ministry on behalf of believers is His personal intercession. (While we understand Christ's work includes being our prophet, priest, and king; it is His work as interceding High Priest that is here in view.)

10. Love is the one trait that God says will mark His children living in this world. (Lead the disciple to identify and define true love.)

MEMORY VERSE:
The Holy Spirit will use John 5:24 throughout the life of the disciple. Act appropriately to ensure the disciple understands the verse in its various facets.

SUPPLEMENTAL MATERIAL & ASSIGNMENT:
Ask for the disciple to share his impression of the article on devotions by George Mueller. After discussing the article, ask that the procedure used by Mueller is exercised during the next week in his personal devotions. Continue to lead in establishing the importance of daily worship by asking the disciple to develop a personal prayer strategy.

One way to set up a strategy is to emphasis a different area of concern each day of the week.

For example: Sunday—personal needs;
Monday—the Church and her leaders;
Tuesday—world evangelism;
Wednesday—missions;
Thursday—all levels of government;
Friday—your employment and co-laborers,
Saturday—family members.

SERMON NOTES:

Continue to check sermon notes—be especially sensitive to how the disciple applies the information and challenge of the messages. Applying God's message in the sermon is essential to spiritual growth.

NOTES

222: The Master's Plan
Session 6

THE FAMILY OF GOD

Assignment for Session 6
 a. Complete: Questions for *The Family of God*
 b. Memorize: John 5:24
 c. Conduct: Daily Devotions
 d. Take: Sermon Notes
 e. Study: the *Church Covenant* on page 75 and 76
 f. Discuss *Planning Sheet* on page 77 and 78 with your Mentor

Introductory Summary: People who trust Christ as Lord and savior are now called the 'Body of Christ.' That term, "Body of Christ," is a spiritual description of the Church's mission in the world. When the "Body" is gathered in Christ's name, it is called the 'Church.' Another designation or description of the Church is 'Family of God.' Let's see what the Word has to say about them.

Questions:

1. Galatians 3:16 uses the word _____ to indicate that we are a part of the family of God. (Compare John 1:12 with Galatians 4:5-6)

2. In II Corinthians 6:17-18, God says that He bears the relationship of _____ to His family.

3. Read John 3:16, John 1:14, and Romans 8:3, and discuss how Jesus is uniquely different as the Son of God from a believer that is called a child of God.

4. In Hebrews 2:11, God says that Jesus is happy to call the rest of God's family His _____.
(Consider also Hebrews 2:17 and Ephesians 3:15. Record your thoughts below.)

5. God says that spiritual birth is given only through Jesus, a fact that guarantees _____ true Lord, _____ faith and _____ baptism (Ephesians 4:4-6). What does this mean to you?

6. Read Ephesians 2:13-22 and discuss what has been broken down.

7. Compare Matthew 16:18 with I Peter 2:4-8; and discuss the analogy that God uses to describe His family.

8. Read Hebrews 10:25, Ecclesiastes 4:9-10; and 1 Peter 3:8 and discuss why it is important that God's children should come together for worship.

9. In Ephesians 2:21-22 and in I Peter 2:5, God refers to His church as a building fitting together. Discuss the importance of this analogy.

10. Read I Corinthians 12:1-11 and fill in the blanks in the following statement: God says that each of His children is given at least one _____ and his_____ is just as important as any other Christian's _____.

11. Using the space below, discuss the significance and meaning of baptism from Romans 6:3-6.

12. Study Luke 22:19-20 and I Corinthians 11:26 and discuss the Lord's Supper.

13. Read Acts 1:8; Matthew 28:19; and Matthew 16:27. Summarize the responsibility of the Christian until Christ comes again.

CHURCH COVENANT

(Here is an example of a covenant being used in many churches.)

Having been led, as we believe, by the Spirit of God, to receive the Lord Jesus Christ as our Savior
And on the profession of our faith, having been baptized in the name of the Father, and of the Son, and of the Holy Ghost,
We do now, in the presence of God, angels, and this assembly, most solemnly and joyfully enter into covenant with one another as one body in Christ.
We engage, therefore, by the aid of the Holy Spirit, to walk together in Christian love; to strive for the advancement of this church, in knowledge, holiness, and comfort;
To promote its prosperity and spirituality; to sustain its worship, ordinances, discipline, and doctrines;
To contribute cheerfully and regularly to the support of the ministry, the expenses for the church, the relief of the poor, and spread of the gospel through all nations.
We also engage to maintain family and secret devotions; to religiously educate our children; to seek the salvation of our kindred and acquaintances;
To walk circumspectly in the world; to be just in our dealings, faithful in our engagements, and exemplary in our deportment;
To avoid all tattling, backbiting, and excessive anger;
To abstain from the sale and use of all substance abuse including intoxicating beverages and to be zealous in our efforts to advance the kingdom of our Savior.
We further engage to watch over one another in brotherly love;
To remember each other in prayer; to aid each other in sickness and distress; to cultivate Christian sympathy in feeling and courtesy in speech;
To be slow to take offense, but always ready for reconciliation, and mindful of the rules of our Savior to secure it without delay.
We moreover engage that when we remove from this place we will, as soon as possible, unite with some other church, where we can carry out the spirit of this covenant and the principles of God's Word.

THE BASIS FOR THE COVENANT

The obligations of church membership outlined in the covenant are all Scriptural,as may be seen from the following study.

Salvation and Baptism
  (John 1:11-12; Matthew 28:19-20)
Duties to the Church
  1. To walk together in Christian love. (John 13:34-35)
  2. To strive for and promote church prosperity and spirituality. (Philippians 1:27; II Timothy 2:15; II Corinthians 7:1; II Peter 3:11)
  3. To sustain its worship, ordinances, discipline, and doctrine. (Hebrews10:25; Matt. 28:19; I Corinthians 11:23-26; Jude 3)
  4. To give it pre-eminence in my life. (Matthew 6:33)
  5. To contribute cheerfully and regularly. (I Corinthians 16:2; II Corinthians 8:6-7)
  6. To carry my membership when I move and be active in church work wherever I live. (Acts 11:19-21; 18:24-28)
Duties in Personal Christian Living
  1. To maintain family and secret devotions. (I Thessalonians 5:17-18; Acts 17:11)
  2. To religiously educate the children. (II Timothy 3:15; Deuteronomy 6:4-7)
  3 To seek the salvation of the lost. (Acts 1:8;Matt. 4:19; Psalm 126:5-6; Proverbs 11:30)
  4. To walk circumspectly in the world, and to be just in our dealings, faithful in our engagements, and exemplary in our deportment. (Ephesians 5:15; Philippians 2:14-15; I Peter 2:11-12)
  5. To avoid gossip and excessive anger. (Ephesians 4:31; I Peter 2:21; Colossians 3:8; James 3:1-2)
  6. To abstain from the sale or use of liquors and other control substances. (Ephesians 5:18; Habakkuk 2:15)
  7. To be zealous in our efforts for Christ (Titus 2:14)
Duties to Fellow Members
  1. To watch over one another in love. (I Peter 1:22)
  2. To pray for one another. (James 5:16)
  3. To aid in sickness and distress. (Galatians 6:2; James 2:14-17)
  4. To cultivate sympathy and courtesy. (I Peter 3:8)
  5. To be slow to take offense, always ready for reconciliation. (Ephesians 4:30-32)

222 PLAN:
WEEKLY PLANNING SHEET

MONTH _____ WEEK OF_____

To Do List:	Weeks Goal:
	Resources Needed:

Action Steps:

222 Plan: Personal Planning

Month_____ Week of: _____

SUNDAY

MONDAY

TUESDAY

WEDNESDAY

THURSDAY

FRIDAY

SATURDAY

Mentor's Guide— Session 6
The Family of God

The believer must now learn to appreciate his new spiritual family. Once God quickens the soul, He awakens us to a new family called "The Church." The church may be referred to as both visible and invisible. The visible church is the local congregation whose members are observed daily, while Christians from all generations comprise the invisible church. She will become visible only in heaven. She will join the angels in singing the praises of God and worship Him forever.

Our interest for now is the local church. God commissioned the visible or existing church to carry out the will of God on earth. Being part of this family requires responsible behavior in keeping with God's instructions. Therefore, the systematic gathering of worshipping believers is the highest form of "Church" activity.

If we lead a disciple into thinking that being a Christian is immersing oneself in church sponsored activity, we would have done the disciple a gross disservice. We would have assured his limited spiritual growth and perverted his concept of God's church. There is nothing wrong with church activities provided they are promoted and led by the Holy Spirit.

However, we must never give the idea that a person is not a good disciple if he doesn't attend all church sponsored functions. We tend to spend time with those we love, not out of obligation but out of a common devotion to the Lord.

The Lord has commanded us to love one another. With these things in mind, lead the disciple to submit to public baptism. Lead him to seek membership in a local church that has a high view of Scripture.

Discuss the following answers and lead the disciple to understand the "Church" through the testimony of Scripture:

1.   The blank should be filled by the word "seed." (Seed is here used to describe the spiritual birth experienced by Christians. Birth is the result of God's seed of Truth being awakened in the soul.)

2.   The term "Father" should fill the blank, and we are to understand that God has received us as His children as we have received His Son as Lord.

3.   Jesus is uniquely the Son of God. He is the only begotten Son. While Christ's son-ship came as a supernatural act of physical conception, our son-ship has come through spiritual adoption.

4.   The Scriptures speak of believers as being brethren of Christ. Christ is our elder brother, and He gladly acknowledges us as His brothers and sisters.

5.   The word "one" repeated three times in the Ephesians passage supports God's unity in His lordship, the spiritual nature of faith, and the importance of baptism as a picture of identification with Christ and His ministry.

6.   The "wall of partition" in the referenced passage speaks of two separations. It speaks first of the separation of man

from God through sin. (Because of sin, the Law becomes an immovable object standing between God and man. God demands perfection of those with whom He would have fellowship. Man is sinful—a breaker of the Law—therefore, if man is to come to God, the wall of separation, "the Law," must be broken down. The secondary reference is to the separation of Jew and Gentile. This "wall" is a separation of prejudice. Christ's death destroyed both walls so that all are equal at the cross. Because of Christ's death as a substitute, anyone receiving Him will be forgiven his violation of God's perfect "Law.")

7. The word "stone" refers to Peter's testimony regarding Christ's divinity. It is upon the work of divine grace that Christ will build His church. Christ is called the chief cornerstone.

8. Attendance at God's assemblies (church) is a command. It is not an option. Our attendance shows our dependence upon Him and builds our faith as we witness others worshipping Him.

9. These verses focus on the unity of the church as Christ's body. Therefore, the church can't properly function without all whom the Father has assigned to her number.

10. The blanks must be filled with "spiritual gift, gift, and gift."

11. Baptism is an act of obedience to Christ. Your purpose is to show your identification with His death, burial, and resurrection. In Christ the believer is dead, buried, and

raised to newness of life. You now possess life that is eternal in quality.

12. The Lord's Supper contains two elements: bread and wine (Wine is fruit juice or fruit of the vine). Bread symbolizes Christ's body broken in death for our sin. The wine symbolizes the shedding of His blood for the forgiveness of sin. The supper reminds us of His sacrifice on our behalf until He comes again.

13. In Christ's absence we should use every honorable means to tell the world of the graciousness of God. We should warn people of God's wrath if Christ is rejected and be quick to tell them of God's forgiveness when Christ is received as Lord
.

WEEKLY DISCIPLINES: Continue all weekly disciplines. Follow the assignment sheet closely. Make sure you check memory verses, sermon notes, etc.

SUPPLEMENTAL MATERIAL & ASSIGNMENT: Following the questions in "Session 6," are two supplemental articles. Assign the reading of the *Church Covenant*. Instruct the disciple to make *Basis of the Covenant* the focus of next week's devotions. You may suggest that he take the points and divide them into six days of devotional reading, meditation, and prayer. It is important that Christians understand their relation and responsibilities to Christ, the Church, and personal holiness.

You will also discover a form titled *Personal Planning Sheet*. Lead the disciple to begin planning the details of life. Christ purposed to die for the sins of the world. All that He did, in His earthly ministry, moved to complete that goal. One may observe this same intensity and discipline in the lives of the apostles. Let the same be said of us. Purposed living is planned living. One way to accomplish purposed living is to observe life as a whole and plans accordingly.

Avoid the temptation to divide the secular from the spiritual. There was no such division in Christ's mind. All of life is sacred. Instruct the disciple to begin using some form of planning guide to show his attempt to give direction and discipline to life's responsibilities.

Some will do better with this assignment than others because of their personalities and natural skills. However, gently press them to be faithful. They will thank you for it later.

NOTES

222: THE MASTER'S PLAN
Session 7

PRAYER

Assignment for Session 7
    a. Complete: Questions for *Prayer*
    b. Memorize: Phillipians 4:6, 7
    c. Conduct: Daily Devotions
    d. Take: Sermon Notes
    e. Discuss: the *Prayer Journal* on page 89 and 90

Introductory Summary: Prayer is that exercise which, when offered in faith, releases the supernatural power of God in our world. Other than the Word of God, nothing is more important in the Christian's life than the consistent exercise of daily prayer. In this study, we will come to grips with some of the issues of prayer.

Questions:

1. Is prayer a Christian option? Answer the question on the basis of Isaiah 55:6, Matthew 7:7, and Philippians 4:6, Explain!

2. Study the "Model Prayer" in Luke 11:1-4 and list the word or phrase that shows the following:

a. Relationship

b. Praise

c. Heavenly Reality

d. Desire for God's Will

e. Sustenance

f. Forgiveness

g. Guidance and Deliverance

Discuss the significance of the pattern Jesus shows in His "model prayer."

3. Review the four passages below about the prayer life of Jesus and fill in your observations under the headings.

Passage	Occasion	Subject of Prayer
John 11:38-44		
Luke 22:39-42		
Luke 23:33-34		
Luke 23:46		

4. Jesus' longest recorded prayer is in John 17. Who was included in this prayer? (Read the whole chapter and note verse 20.)

5. What was Jesus' prayer for His disciples in John 17:25-26?

6. The Bible teaches us numerous principles for effective prayer. List the principles taught in each of the following references.

    a.   Matthew 6:14-15

    b.   John 14:13-14

    c.   John 15:7

    d.   James 1:5-6

    e.   James 4:2-3

    f.   James 5:16

    g.   I John 3:22

    h.   Psalm 66:18; Isaiah 59:2

7. Study Philippians 4:6-7 very carefully and record your observations regarding the why, how, and result of prayer.

222 Plan: Prayer Journal

DATE	PRAYER REQUEST

222 Plan: Prayer Journal

DATE	PRAYER REQUEST

Mentor's Guide— Session 7
Prayer

Prayer is the one Christian discipline you must build into the disciple's life. If this discipline is not practiced daily, the Christian heart will become dehydrated. The disciple's spiritual fortune will rise, or fall based on the effectiveness of his prayer life. Therefore, be sensitive to your disciple's needs for developing a prayer life. Jesus prayed that believers would know the love He had experienced with His Father. He also prayed for the Spirit of God to be in them.

1.   The Christian has no option in prayer. It is commanded by the Lord, and He meets the believer in this special bonding of hearts in communion.

2.   The model prayer has at least seven ingredients:

Relationship	—"Our Father"
Praise	—"hallowed be Thy name"
Heavenly reality	—"which art in heaven"
Desire for God's will	—"Thy will be done"
Sustenance	—"give us this day our daily bread"
Forgiveness	—"forgive us our trespasses"
Deliverance	—"deliver us from evil"

3.   The prayers of Jesus—note the following occasions:

John 11:38-44	Lazarus' death	Jesus prayed people would believe God sent Him.
Luke 22:39-42	Mt. of Olives	Jesus prayed for the will of God to be done.

| Luke 23:33-34 | Crucifixion | Jesus prayed for those who crucified Him. |
| Luke 23:46 | Christ's Death | Jesus prayed His Father would receive His Spirit. |

4. In John 17, Jesus prayed for Himself, His disciples, and those who would believe in generations to come.

5. Jesus prayed that believers would know the love He had experienced with His Father. He also prayed for the Spirit of God to be in them.

6. The conditions for effective prayer are:
    a. Conditioned upon our forgiving those who sin against us. (Matt. 6:14-15)
    b. Conditioned upon the will of God. (When believers pray, using the seal of His name, we dare not ask for anything that would not bless the Lord. We can ask boldly where we have the authority of His Word—knowing it to be His will.) (John 14:13-14)
    c. Conditioned upon our abiding in Him. (John 15:7)
    d. Conditioned upon our praying in faith.(James 1:5,6)
    e. Conditioned upon proper requests. (James 4:2--3)
    f. Conditioned upon confession of sin. (James 5:16)
    g. Conditioned upon keeping His commandments. (I John 3:22)
    h. Conditioned upon repentance. (Psalm 66:18; Isaiah 59:2)

7. Your disciple should have come to an understanding that closely resembles the following statements:
(1) "The believer's prayer petitions are made with thanksgiving and without anxiousness."

(2) "Anxiety reveals a lack of faith in God's ability or desires to fulfill our needs."
WEEKLY DISCIPLINES: Continue all weekly disciplines. Follow the assignment sheet closely. Make sure you check memory verses, sermon notes, etc.

SUPPLEMENTAL MATERIAL & ASSIGNMENT:
Use the Personal Prayer Record form found following the seventh session to record prayers and God's responses.

NOTES

222: THE MASTER'S PLAN
Session 8

THE HOLY SPIRIT

Assignments for Session 8:
  a. Complete: Questions for *The Holy Spirit*
  b. Memorize: Galatians 5:22, 23
  c. Conduct: Daily Devotions
  d. Take: Sermon Notes
  e. Study: *Disciples Life Chart* on page 99

Introductory Summary: The Holy Spirit is the third person of the trinity. He is God, and equals with the Father, and the Son. The believer must learn how to honor the Father, and the Son, through the Spirit.

Questions:

1. Read I John 5:7, and record the three entities that are one.

2. The Holy Spirit is a distinct person with an individual personality. Review the following Scriptures and discern the personality traits depicted in them:

  a. Romans 8:27

  b. I Corinthians 12:1

  c. Ephesians. 4:30

3. The Holy Spirit made it possible for you to see your sinful condition and confess Jesus as your Lord and Savior. He did this by:

(1) _____ of sin (John 16:8) and

(2) _____ Jesus (I Corinthians 12:3).

4. Read Romans 8:9, John 14:17, and I Corinthians 3:16 and discuss what the Holy Spirit does when you willingly receive Jesus.

5. The Holy Spirit performs a great many functions and serves a lot of purposes within the believer's life. Review the following verses and for each one, record the appropriate purpose or action the Holy Spirit accomplishes on behalf of the believer.

a. Ephesians 1:14

b. John 14:26

c. Romans 8:16

d. Acts 10:19

e. Romans 8:26-27

6.   The Christian whose life is sincerely yielded to God finds that the Holy Spirit is continuously producing good, wholesome fruit in his life. Read John 15:5 and Gal. 5:22 and list manifestations of the fruit of the Holy Spirit.

7.   In the following verses, is a list of suggested the checkpoints we should use if he desiring to be filled with the Holy Spirit. Ponder these in your heart.
   a.   Repent of sin! (Acts 2:38)
   b.   Long or thirst for God! (John 7:37-38)
   c.   Yield obedience to God! (Acts 5:32)
   d.   Pray for the Holy Spirit's filling! (Luke 11:13)
   e.   Believe that God hears and answers your plea! (I John 5:14-15)

Do you agree with the list? Explain.

Additional reading for more enlightenment:
      John 14:16-26
      Acts 2
      Romans 8

NOTES

THE DISCIPLES LIFE

MAY BE SEEN AS THE FOUR BALANCED SECTIONS OF A CIRCLE OR WHEEL.

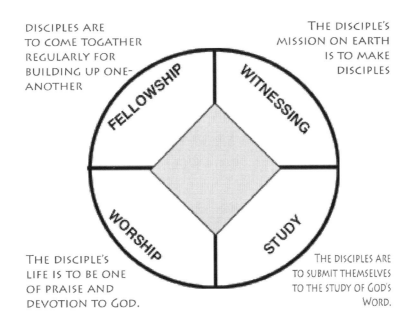

DISCIPLES ARE TO COME TOGATHER REGULARLY FOR BUILDING UP ONE-ANOTHER

THE DISCIPLE'S MISSION ON EARTH IS TO MAKE DISCIPLES

FELLOWSHIP

WITNESSING

WORSHIP

STUDY

THE DISCIPLE'S LIFE IS TO BE ONE OF PRAISE AND DEVOTION TO GOD.

THE DISCIPLES ARE TO SUBMIT THEMSELVES TO THE STUDY OF GOD'S WORD.

A BALANCED LIFE IS ESSENTIAL

A BALANCED LIFE COMES AS A DISCIPLE ABIDES IN CHRIST IN ALL FOUR QUADRANTS OF THE CIRCLE ABOVE.

DESIGN BY: W. L. OWENS

NOTES

Mentor's Guide— Session 8
The Holy Spirit

The ministry of the Holy Spirit is often misunderstood. You have an opportunity to help correct the problem by working with your disciple. We must not assume that we have all the answers about the Holy Spirit's ministry, but we must be Biblical with our answers. Being Biblical means we look at the Scriptures through the lens of His revelation instead of the lens of our own biases. What we think about the Holy Spirit must be brought in line with what the Bible actually teaches about Him. Therefore, lead your disciple carefully through these basic considerations about the Holy Spirit.

1.   The three persons of the Godhead are: Father, Son, and Holy Spirit. All three are mentioned in 1 John 5:7. (Scholars disagree about the authenticity of the verse. Please note, that the Truth here taught is supported throughout the Scriptures. Therefore, the doctrine of the trinity does not depend on the verse in question.)

2.   The Holy Spirit's personality is seen in the following:

Romans 8:27: The Holy Spirit makes intercession for us according to God's will. (He knows our mind, and the mind of the Father.)

1 Corinthians 12:1: The Holy Spirit's personality is seen when He gives spiritual gifts. Only a personal being can give gifts.

Ephesians 4:30: The Holy Spirit has emotions and can be grieved by our sin. Expression of emotion is a personality trait. When believers sin, the Holy Spirit is grieved and withdraws His fellowship until one repents confesses and asks for forgiveness.

3.   The blanks should be filled with the words "conviction" and "confess."

4.   When one sincerely repents and turns to Christ as Lord, the Holy Spirit comes into his life to reside. The indwelling Spirit ministers to and through the believer in the world.

5.   The Holy Spirit ministers in specific ways as indicated in the following verses: (The list is not exhaustive!)

Ephesians 1:14: The verse paints a legal picture of the Holy Spirit guaranteeing the final fulfillment of God's design for His children.

John 14:26: He is the counselor who will teach believers the teachings of Jesus.

Romans 8:16: He bears testimony to our spirits that we are the children of God.

Acts 10:19: He communicates the will of God to the believer.

Romans 8:26-27: He helps us in our weakness.

6.   The Christian, whose life is filled with the Spirit of God, will—to some degree—show the following traits:

love, joy, peace, long suffering, gentleness, goodness, faith, meekness, and temperance.

7. Review the issues related to the filling of the Spirit with the disciple. Please take note of the following observations:

Acts 2:38: The fullness of the Spirit comes when we are emptied of sin through repentance and confession.

John 7:37, 38: Only the thirsty continue to drink of the water of life. (Let us ask for God to make us thirsty.)

Acts 5:32: When we yield our wills in obedience, He gives us the fullness of the Spirit. (Spirit fullness equals Spirit control. Therefore, it follows that those who are controlled by the Spirit are filled by the Spirit.)

Luke 11:13: While many teach that the Christian does not need to ask for the Holy Spirit, there is a sense in which it is always right to ask for God to grant you a sensitivity to His reality. However, there may be times when it will please God to have you walk by faith and not by sight or feelings.

I John 5:14, 15: God promises to answer the prayers of those who petition Him on the basis of His will and the honor of His name. The Spirit-filled believer is one who knows the mind of God and prays in accordance with that knowledge.

WEEKLY DISCIPLINES: Continue all weekly disciplines. Follow the assignment sheet closely. Make sure you check memory verses, sermon notes, etc.

SUPPLEMENTAL MATERIAL & ASSIGNMENT:
Determine if the suggested additional reading was accomplished. Then, ask for a synopsis of each passage. The disciple should be ready to discuss the chart: *The Disciple's Life*. Expect an explanation of the chart and a personal evaluation of how well his life measures up in each of the four areas.

222: THE MASTER'S PLAN
Session 9

ABIDING IN CHRIST

Assignment for Session 9

    a. Complete: Exercise for *Abiding in Christ*
    b. Memorize: John 15:5
    c. Conduct: Daily Devotions
    d. Take: Sermon Notes
    e. Study: *Goforth's 7 Rules* page 111

Introductory Summary: If we are to be successful in living for Christ, it is essential that we understand our need to abide in Him. To abide means to rest—a life of obedience to Christ is impossible without resting in Him. His resources are available as we abide in Him. In preparation for the following study, read John 15 in several translations.

Questions:

1. According to John 15:5 what is the result of abiding in Christ?

2. We need to understand what it means to "abide in Christ." Give true/false answers to the following: Circle One!

    a.   Christ has come into the believer's heart and has is the Lord of life. Therefore, believers belong to Christ (1 Corinthians 3:23; Romans 14:8). T F

    b.   To abide means to continue following Christ day after day or to be steadfast (Colossians 1:2-5; John 8:31; Acts 2:42). T F

    c.   To abide in Christ means to be with Him or to walk through life with Him (Colossians 2:6). T F

    d.   To abide in Christ means to have your spiritual desires fulfilled (John 15:7). T F

    e.   To abide in Christ means to metaphorically feed continuously on Jesus (John 6:56). T F
(A metaphor is an expression designed to carry a mental picture. In this passage, the believer is challenged to feed upon the "Truth" of Jesus to satisfy spiritual hunger as one would feed upon flesh to satisfy physical hunger.)

    f.   To abide in Christ means to spiritually hear the voice of Christ (John10:27). T F

    g.   To abide in Christ means to be dead to the old nature and to be alive with a new or spiritual nature (2 Corinthians 5:17; Galatians 2:20). T F

h. To abide in Christ means to be continually identified with Him (John 3:21). T F

(Baptism is a form of identification. The Jews were often baptized to identify with being cleansed from sin. Some were baptized to identify with a message declared by a prophet, such as John the Baptist. Christians in this present time are baptized to show identity with the death, burial, and resurrection of Christ. Identification, of this form, is often likened unto the Jews being identified with Jehovah through circumcision.) (Romans 6:1-4)

i. To abide in Christ means to love your fellowman (1 John 4:7, 12). T F

j. To keep His commandments, means to abide in Christ (1 John 3:24). T F

k. To abide in Christ is likened unto to being an obedient bride of Christ (Romans 7:4). T F

3. When abiding in Christ the Christian has many rich rewards. Look up the following verses and fill in the blanks.

a. He will bear_____(John 15:5).

b. He will have whatever he _____granted (John 15:7,16).

c. He will be happy when _____returns (1 John 2:28).

d. He will be_____in the midst of trouble (John 16:33).

e. He has a _____ life (2 Corinthians 5:17).

f. He has a righteousness that comes through _____ (Philippians 3:9).

g. He has the_____to teach him (John 14:26; 1 John 2:27).

4. As Christ abides in His Father, we must abide in Him (John 17:20, 21). T or F?

5. Faith in Christ is essential before Christ can abide in a person and that person abide in Christ (Ephesians 3:17-19). T or F?

6. Failure to abide in Christ has many negative consequences for the person who professes to be a follower of Christ. Look up the following:

a. No spiritual _____ can be born (John 15:4).

b. There is a danger of being unusable to_____ (Matthew 3:9-10, Hebrews 6:7-8).

c. Worldly things _____ out the good seed of God's eternal Word (Matthew 13:22).

d. It brings disappointment to the_____ hearted (Luke 13:6-9).

e. Life's _____and resources are wasted
    and not invested for God (Luke 11-23).

7. Obedience is required to abide in Christ. Deliberately
seeking after Christ and heeding His commandments en-
ables us to abide in Him. Some of the things that must
command your time and attention are included in the following verses. Refer to each one and complete the blank
statements.

a. Christ will make each of you a _____of_____
    (Matthew 4:19).

b. Meditate or ponder the _____ of Christ
    (Psalms 1:2).

c. Let your_____ dwell on wholesome things
    (Philippians 4:8).

d. Let every one of your activities be done for God's
    _____(1 Corinthians 10:31).

e. Keep on_____spiritually instead of trying
    to coast along (1 Peter 2:2).

f. Let seeking after_____, be the goal of
    your life (Matthew 6:33).

g. Be conscious of your _____being the
    temple of the Spirit (1 Corinthians 6; 19-20).

h. Be ready for the_____ of Christ
    (Matthew 24:44).

NOTES

GOFORTH'S SEVEN RULES FOR DAILY LIVING
(Written on the fly leaf of his Bible)

1. Seek to give much—expect nothing.

2. Put the very best construction on the actions of others.

3. Never let a day pass without at least a quarter of an hour spent in the study of the Bible.

4. Never omit daily morning and evening private prayers and devotions.

5. In all things seek to know God's will, and when known obey at any cost.

6. Seek to cultivate a quiet, prayerful spirit.

7. Seek each day to do or say something to further Christianity among the heathen.

(Jonathan Goforth was greatly used of God to light fires of spiritual awakening as a missionary.)

NOTES

Mentor's Guide— Session 9
Abiding In Christ

We now move into another area of Christian discipline—learning to abide in Christ. Do not allow the disciple to proceed until he has meditatively read John 15. If the assignment has not been properly completed, simply have prayer and terminate the session. Continue the next week only when the assignment has been completed.

All the True/False questions are true. There is a pedagogical reason for putting forth the questions in this manner. Truth is being propositionally stated. To avoid confusion, when dealing with new Christians, we want to state principles as facts of truth. Some will soon discover the trend and will be tempted not to look up the passages for the answer. To circumvent this potential problem go over each T/F answer asking why each one is true. (From this process, you will teach them it is not only important to have the right answer but also to know why the answer is correct.)

1. John 15:5 states that those who abide in Christ will bear much fruit.

2. As stated above, all statements in this question are true.

3. The abiding believer will: (The fill-in for each blank is in parentheses.)
   a. bear (much fruit).
   b. have his (desires) granted. (Help the disciple to understand these desires must be in the will of God.)
   c. be happy when (Christ) returns.

    d. be (peaceful) in the midst of trouble.
    e. have a (new) life.
    f. have a righteousness that comes through (faith).
    g. have the (Holy Spirit) to teach him.

4. True. Why? It is only in Christ that we are made part of God's family.

5. True. Why? The family bond is not established without faith or trust.

6. The blank spaces in this question should be filled in as follows: Words meaning the same thing are acceptable. Make sure the disciple understands the principles involved.
    a. fruit
    b. God
    c. choke
    d. the hungry
    e. materials

7. The blank spaces in this question should be as follows:
    a. fisher of men
    b. law
    c. thoughts
    d. glory
    e. growing
    f. God
    g. body
    h. coming

SUPPLEMENTAL MATERIAL & ASSIGNMENT:

Continue the activities of Scripture memory, intercessory prayer, Bible study, and sermon note taking. Be sure to check on the assignments. Even Christians will have a tendency to let go what you do not inspect. Remind your disciple that he is responsible for referring to the assignment sheet to ensure his compliance.

Go over *Goforth's Seven Rules for Daily Living* with your disciple. Be sure to emphasize that one would do well to make these rules a minimum goal for daily living.

(Go over the assignment for the next session and make sure the various items assigned are understood. Pray with your disciple and encourage him where progress is observed.)

NOTES

222: THE MASTER'S PLAN
Session 10

CHASTENING AND PRUNING

Assignment for Session 10
- a. Complete: Questions for *Chastening & Pruning*
- b. Memorize: Hebrews 12:6
- c. Conduct: Daily Devotions
- d. Take: Sermon Notes

Introductory Summary: There is much confusion concerning the child of God who allows himself to be drawn into sin. Our purpose now, is to show God's love through discipline.

When a believer sins, God does not abandon him. However, He disciplines him that he may grow in the stature and knowledge of the Lord Jesus Christ.

Questions:

1. We need to understand some things concerning the individual believer himself. He has newly inherited benefits through the things that Christ has done, and is doing, for him. Look up the following verses of Scripture and fill in the blanks:
- a. There is only one who is _____ (Luke 18:19).

b. The saved person has no _____ of his own.
    He has an imputed _____ from Jesus
    (Romans 4:21-25).

c. Believers have been given the right to become
    _____ of God. (John 1:12-13)

d. The saved person now has God's Spirit to help him
    do the right thing, but the child of God stumbles
    and commits _____ at times (Ps. 51:1-4;
    1 John 1:8-9).

e. When the child of God does stumble he is not cast
    down or out of God's family (Ps. 37:23-24).
    T or F

f. When Jesus died on the cross He was the_____
    of God. (John 1:29; Romans 5:6-8).

    (Note: The animal being sacrificed in the temple
    [once each year] became a substitute for the sins
    of the people of Israel. When Jesus died for the sins
    of the world, He became the substitute sin offering
    for all people who receive Him as Lord and Savior.)

g. The _____ of Jesus cleanses the child of
    God from the guilt of his sins (I John 1:7).

h. Jesus is continually interceding before_____
    on behalf of His sheep (people). His intercession is
    essential for forgiveness of the believer's sin
    (I John 2:1).

2.   God hates sin and consequently cannot allow sin to go without judgment (Acts 17:30; Hebrews 9:27). T or F

3.   God's purpose is to develop His children into Christ's likeness and, therefore, must correct or chastise them when they _____ (Hebrews 12:6; Deuteronomy 8:5).

4.   The chastening of God shows definite_____ and concern for His children (Hebrews 12:6).

5.   As His children, Christians should not be rebellious or give up as God chastens (Hebrews12:5). T or F

6.   The very nature of chastening or the pruning away of undesirable qualities within us may be likened unto a surgeon removing a cancerous tumor. Therefore, chastening is a distasteful but necessary process. (Hebrews 12:11). T or F

7.   God has in mind some definite qualities that He wants developed in his children. He wishes to use them in this world for His own glory. Look up the following passages and complete the sentences:

   a.   God desires that His children _____
        regarding any self-centered ambitions
        (John 12:24-25).

   b.   God wants us to _____Him supremely
        above all other loves (Luke 14:26).

        (Note: The verse cited shows how serious Jesus is
        about the need for unwavering commitment to Him.
        Our love for family would be like hate in contrast

to our love and commitment to Him.)

c. In service to Christ, His child is to _____
all that he has (Luke 14:33).

d. Christians are to remain steadfast in God's_____
(John 8:31).

e. God's children must bear _____
(John 15:8).

8. When God's children have submitted to His chastening without getting bitter or discouraged, they will afterward see the good that has come out of the experience. Look up the following verses and record the results of allowing yourself to be corrected by God:

a. Hebrews 12:11

b. Romans 5:3

c. Romans 5:4

d. Hebrews 12:6

f. John 15:2

9. Study Hebrews 6:4-6 and record your conclusions below. Remember, however, that the overwhelming testimony of Scripture is that the child of God is safe in Jesus.
There are three common interpretations and applications of the passage:
(1). The writer is referring to true believers who reject

Christ and fall away, losing their salvation.

(2). The writer is presenting a hypothetical situation that cannot happen. But if it were to happen, then there would be the loss of the believer's salvation.

(3). The writer is referring to those who have professed Christ, but in reality have not been accepted by Him and their falling away proves their state.

In the space below, state which of the above is the correct interpretation and Why? (Do you have another interpretation?) (If the Hebrews passage referenced above is confusing to you, seek counsel. Both mentor and disciple may need to spend an extra session working through this passage until you both have peace from God regarding your understanding.)

NOTES

Mentor's Guide – Session 10
Chastening and Pruning

Christians must understand that God does not intend for us to live lives free from pain and disappointment. Believers often conceive the idea that being a Christian eliminates trouble in life. The Christian life, while filled with the joy of devotion, is also affected by attacks by the enemy and the discipline of the Lord.

We now seek to address the issue of God's work in the life of the sinning Christian. Often, when sin enters the believers life, he feels lost and without a spiritual compass. He wonders what God is doing in His life. One thing is for sure —God never abandons His people, nor will He tolerate their sin.

1. By looking up the designated passages the disciple will discover some Bible facts about himself and God. (The words beside the letters are the answers to fill blanks.)
    a. good
    b. righteous, righteousness
    c. children
    d. sin
    e. True
    f. lamb
    g. blood
    h. the Father (God)

2. True! Why? Because He is holy, and all sin must be judged. Sin will not escape judgment. Those who refuse to

separate themselves from sin must suffer the judgment of sin. The only hope for our separation from sin is the death of Jesus as our substitute.

3.   The blank should be filled with the word "sin." The references deal with the act of God correcting His children. God's purpose in chastisement is that we cease our sins and walk in the power of His presence. While sin is active in the believer's life, God will not bless him with an awareness of His presence or His fellowship. This condition does not mean that God has removed salvation. It means that God will not bless the believer with a sense of assurance until he has repented and confessed his sin.

4.   "Love" is the key word. (Discuss the note following the sentence with the "blank.")

5.   True! Why? Because we have His promise that what He does is best for us.

6.   True

7.   The following passages reveal the qualities God is developing in His children:
   a.   John12:24, 25   —die (death to self)
   b.   Luke14:26   —love
   c.   Luke14:33   —forsake (forsaking self)
   d.   John8:31   —Word
   e.   John15:8   —fruit

8.   The results of God's correction produce the following results in the Christian's life:
   a.   Peace

b. Patience
c. Experience
d. Hope
e. Assurance
f. More fruit

9. These verses in Hebrews 6 are controversial. If taken alone and without the consideration of other Scripture, one might draw the conclusion that believers may lose the salvation of God. Study the text and share the fruit of your study with your disciple.

SUPPLEMENTAL MATERIALS & ASSIGNMENTS:
Make sure you have an understanding about next week's assignment. Reaffirm your instructions are understood by asking the disciple to share with you what he believes his assignment to be. Check on all assigned material. Remember, people do what you inspect.

Don't forget to close your time together in prayer.

NOTES

222: THE MASTER'S PLAN
Session 11

CONFESSION OF SIN

Assignment for Session 11:
 a. Complete: Questions for *Confession of Sin*
 b. Memorize: Review all Verses
 c. Conduct: Daily Devotions
 d. Take: Sermon Notes

Introductory Summary: when considering salvation, confession of sin is often minimized or even overlooked. When studying the Scriptures, it becomes obvious that God places a premium on recognizing and confessing ones sin. You cannot confess sin if you do not "see" the sin.

Questions:

1. Read Psalm 51:1-5 and record your understanding of the significance of David's contrition.

2. In Leviticus 5:5 God requires that a man shall _____ his sin. (Discuss your answer in the space below.)

3. In such passages as Job 33:26-30 and I John 1:8, 9 one can discern that God listens for us to confess our sins.
 T or F

4. In Joshua 7:19, Jeremiah 3:13, and James 5:16, man is exhorted to confess his sin. T or F

5. Read Leviticus 26:40-42 and Proverbs 28:13 and list the promises God makes to those who confess their sins. (Discuss the significance of your discovery in the space below.)

6. According to the Word of God, confession of sin should be accompanied by the following: (Draw a line matching the item in the left-hand column with the correct Scripture verse.)

    a. Submission to punishment   —Leviticus 26:40-42

    b. Prayer for forgiveness   —Numbers 5:6,7

    c. Self-abasement   —Psalm 38:18

    d. Godly sorrow   —Proverb 28:13

    e. Forsaking sin   —Isaiah 64:5,6

    f. Restitution   —II Samuel 24:10

7. Psalm 106:6 indicates that confession of sin should be full and unreserved. T or F

8. After we have confessed our sin, what does God promise in accordance with 1 John 1:9?

9. Write a summary of your understanding of what the Bible teaches about the relationship between the confession of our sins and God's forgiveness.

NOTES

Mentor's Guide—Session 11
Confession of Sin

The spiritual discipline of moment-by-moment confession of sin is sorely missing in today's catalog of Christian experience. It is precisely this discipline that allows the believer to know the fullness and satisfaction of walking with God. Lead your disciple to appreciate how essential the act of true confession is to his spiritual health and service.

1.   When you consider the disciple's response to this first question,Look for evidence of his insight into the true nature of confession and contrition. If he doesn't understand, his spiritual growth will be stunted. The issue is so important that you may need to ask, "Is he really born again?"

2.   The answer is "confess," ask: "What it means to confess?"(Confession is more than just expressing the verbal fact that one has sinned. Confession involves repentance and, by the grace of God, taking a genuine stand against the sin.)

3.   True! Why? Because, the evidence bears testimony to God being at work in the circumstances of life. His convicting work brings us to the place of confession. It is only when we confess that God grants His forgiveness and restores the "joy" of salvation.

4.   True

5.   Upon confession, God promised to remember His covenant with Abraham, Isaac, and Jacob. He further promised to extend His mercy when sin is confessed. These

truths also affect believers in this present generation. While God has not given salvation provisionally, He has made our fellowship with Him contingent upon our obedience.

6. The subjects should be matched to the following Scriptures:

Submission to punishment	Leviticus 26:41
Self-abasement	Isaiah 64:5,6
Godly sorrow	Psalm 38:18
Forsaking sin	Proverbs 28:13
Restitution	Numbers 5:6,7

7. True

8. God promises forgiveness and cleansing for those who confess their sin.

9. Your disciple should convey an assurance that God really means business when dealing with sin. Although the wrath of God burns hotly against all sin, God's mercy is just as thorough when applied to those who confess and forsake their sin. Just a word on forsaking sin—because the sin principle is at work in us, it is impossible for us to guarantee the Lord that we will not commit the sin again. Why, because even "born again" people have a sinful nature and will sin if they do not follow the Holy Spirit. The passages in I John, chapters one and two, form a Biblical commentary on how God provides for failure in the Christian life.

SUPPLEMENTAL MATERIALS & ASSIGNMENTS:
Refer to the assignment sheet and make sure all items have been completed. Don't overlook the sermon notes and the

prayer strategy. Check on your disciple's progress in recording his spiritual insight.

Follow a routine when checking assignments. It is easy to assume people have done what you have assigned. If they get the idea that you are not holding them accountable, they will begin to yield to the temptation to let it slide. Your disciple must understand that the building of these disciplines is a key to his usefulness to God.

NOTES

222: THE MASTER'S PLAN
Session 12

CLEANSING FROM SIN

Assignment for Session 12:
  a. Complete: Questions for *Cleansing from Sin*
  b. Memorize: I John 1:8, 9
  c. Conduct: Daily Devotions
  d. Take: Sermon Notes
  e. Study: *Hints for Worker's* page 139

Introductory Summary: The principles of cleansing and confessing are very closely related. We have just finished a study on confession of sin. Now let us turn our attention to the cleansing which is received upon confession. Job asked the question, "Who can bring a clean thing out of an unclean?" The obvious answer is "God." Only God can cleanse a sinner from the effects of his sin.

Questions:

1. The above quotation came from Job___: ___. (Using a concordance, look up the word "unclean" and identify the chapter and verse.)

2. It is necessary that we are cleansed from the effects of sin because there are three enemies that work against the Christian to bring defilement to his life. Look up the following verses and identify these enemies.

   a. Galatians 1:4

   b. II Corinthians 12:7

   c. Galatians 5:17

3. Sin brings certain consequences into the believer's life. Some of these are: fellowship with God is broken; prayer becomes a formality; Bible study becomes a chore, etc., Can you think of other consequences because of sin in the believer's life?

4. God has not left the believer without a provision for cleansing from his sin. Job did not know the answer to the questions he asked. However, God has shown through principles in the Bible a threefold provision. Look up the following verses of Scripture and complete the blanks: John 15:3, I John 1:7-9.

   a. The _____ cleanses.

   b. The _____ of Christ cleanses.

   c. The Holy Spirit cleanses.
   (By deduction, we know that the Holy Spirit is active in the cleansing process. Based on your understanding of the Bible, describe below how you feel He is used by God to bringing cleansing to the Christian's life.)

5. The cleansing process requires certain action. The following lists the required action for daily cleansing: (Match the verses with the proper response by drawing a line from the verse to the response.)

I John 1:9a   Recognize the holiness of God

Psalm 103:   Be honest about your sins

I John 1:9b   Confess your sins to God

I Peter 1:16   By Faith receive the cleansing He has promised

I John 1:6   Forsake and forget your sins.

Our Lord has provided for daily cleansing. If one does not accept His provision, he cannot experience the Spirit anointed life.

Without practicing the principle of cleansing, one cannot become the salt of the earth.

NOTES

HINTS FOR WORKERS

By Jessie Penn-Lewis

(Suggested Instructions by W. L. Owens for using this article)

Over the next twelve days, focus on the following twelve paragraphs in your devotions. Look up the verses referenced and meditate upon the meaning. Ask God to make the subject of each section a reality in your life. Resist the temptation to do more than one paragraph each day, because, you need time for spiritual attrition to take place.

While Jessie Penn-Lewis wrote the article to address Christians in vocational "ministry," it is applicable for all Christians because all believers are priests and ministers for God.

"God's fellow-workers" (I Corinthians 3:9), who "watch (for) souls as those that shall give account" (Hebrews 13:17) *

1.   **Seek to meet souls on their own level,** and to look at difficulties from their standpoint (I Corinthians 9:22). Give them sympathy (I Peter 3:8); gently lead their thoughts away from the human to the Divine side. Give them encouragement and do not cast them down (I Thessalonians 2:11, and 5:14). Always teach them that the ground of their peace is the blood of Christ, not their feelings or experiences.

2.   **Seek to be but a "voice" used to direct souls to Christ.** Be willing to pass out of sight and be forgotten, and do not allow your thoughts to dwell upon the honor of being "used". (See II Corinthians 12:15; John 1:37; John 3:26-30.)

3.   **Fear the human impress upon the souls you help,** for that must pass away; and covet to be but an instrument through whom the Spirit of God can work unhindered (Colossians 1:29; Romans 15:18).

4.   **Seek for grace to discern the working of God in souls,** so as to cooperate with Him, and to be able to wait with, and for Him, in His "long patience" (James 5:7). Fear to

push souls beyond their measure and thus hinder His work in them. (See Isaiah 42:3,4; II Corinthians 6:1) Pray for heavenly wisdom to know the "grace" wherein a soul stands experimentally (Romans 5:2), that you may lead it on to the next stage. Never scold it for not "seeing" all at once. God is tender with His children and "lures" not forces them on (Job 36:16. See John 16:12, and I Corinthians 3:2)

5. Seek earnestly to know the "silence of Jesus", and never talk of "where people are" in their spiritual growth. The "measuring rod" is for ourselves (as to our limits), not others (II Corinthians 10:12-17). Given diligence to cultivate the unity of the Spirit and do not dwell upon "divisions " pour out the love of God upon all who appear to misjudge you. Enter into the interests of others (Romans 15:2) and be fervent in prayer and silent in speech over all un-Christ-likeness (I Peter 4:8).

6. Seek to manifest that lowliness of mind which makes it easy to take the lowest place (Phillipians 2:3). Never argue nor enter into discussions that "gender strife" (II Timothy 2:23). Note the symptoms of the soul-sickness described in I Timothy 6:4, that you may not "minister questions, rather than godly edifying" (I Timothy 1:4).

7. Do not dogmatize over anything, much less "doubtful" things, nor be anxious to press others to walk by your light. (Note I Corinthians 7:17.) Lead souls to search the written Word to know the mind of the Spirit for themselves. God will teach honest souls. Give credit to others for integrity of heart in desiring to do the will of God (See Romans 14:1).

8. Seek to live in unbroken communion with God, so that there will be a continuous inflow of Divine life to quicken all past knowledge of His Truth. Light without life is our danger. Witnesses are needed to tell out what they know, not what they think; to such testimony the Spirit will bear witness also (John 15:26,27), and the letter of the Word will not merely lodge in the intellect of others, but sink into the heart and spring forth into life eternal (II Corinthians 3:6).

9. If we teach from last week's experience without the fresh life of God passing through us today, we shall become as "sounding brass", empty and powerless; but if we draw direct from the Living Lord, He will make use of our capabilities, old experiences, and knowledge. A very different thing to our making use of them, and depending upon them instead of upon Him. (See Leviticus 26:10.)

10. The soul that is an "instrument" has nothing to "maintain"; it does not cling to "views", nor seek to fight for God. It prefers not to say "I think", nor "This is my opinion," lest it should intrude between God and others; therefore it says "It is written" and leaves the rest to Him. (See the attitude of the Lord Jesus in John 7:16,17.)

11. The interior and exterior life should correspond. It is therefore unwise to be absorbed in the "deep things of God" to the neglect of practical duties, and the winning of souls. Others have a right to gauge our "spirituality" by our "practicality". See I Corinthians 2:10; Ephesians 4:1,2; I Thessalonians 2:12; II Corinthians 6:4-9; I Peter 2:12.

12. Above all things press on to know God, and the deepest meaning of the life hid with Christ in God, leaving behind all craving for emotional experiences and "manifestations". (See Philippians 3:10, 13, 14.) Let your ceaseless position, as to the past be: "I have been crucified with Christ" (Galatians 2:20) whilst moment by moment, under the cleansing blood, you "Present yourselves unto God, as ALIVE from the dead, and your members as INSTRUMENTS" (Romans 6:13). *References from Revised Version (1881-85)

NOTES

Mentor's Guide—Session 12
Cleansing From Sin

Repentance, confession, cleansing and forgiveness are all related. Some believe these four concepts are part of a process, even to the point that you cannot have one without the others. In this "accountability session," you must focus on the Biblical concept of cleansing as it relates to the Biblical view of repentance, confession, etc.

For example, the Bible mentions repentance that is not unto godly sorrow. A person possessing such repentance has not known Biblical repentance and, therefore, is not considered to be repentant at all. If a person has not experienced Biblical repentance which in turn results in genuine confession, he cannot enter the experience of divine cleansing from his sin.

Be sensitive to the above concepts as you seek insight into your disciple's heart. If he doesn't understand, keep going over the applicable Scriptures until the light floods his soul.

1. Job 14:4 (Be sure you demonstrate how one uses a concordance.)

2. The agents that induce us to defile ourselves are:
    a. The world (Galatians 1:4).
    b. The devil (II Corinthians 12:7).
    c. The flesh (Galatians 5:17).

3. Note the suggestions of your disciple and check the answers for accuracy. (If the item or items are not a result of sin, gently show how the error was made.)

4. The blanks "a" and "b" are filled with "Word" and "blood." These two words are symbolic of a spiritual reality that provides the believer with a sense of being cleansed from the guilt of sin. (The Holy Spirit applies the supernatural elements used in cleansing.)

5. The following verses and phrases should follow the pattern below:
    a. I John 1:9   Confess your sins to God
    b. Psalm 103:1   Forsake & forget your sin
    c. I John 1:9b   Receive cleansing by faith
    d. I Peter 1:16   Recognize the holiness of God
    e. I John 1:6   Be honest about your sin

Be sure your disciple has an understanding of the relationship between confession, forgiveness, and cleansing. Before leading this session, study thoroughly all your available resources for clarity.

SUPPLEMENTAL MATERIALS & ASSIGNMENT:
The article *Hints For Workers* must be studied in detail. I suggest that you have your disciple make it the centerpiece of next week's devotional time. For example, have them meditatively read two sections of the article each day. Have them look up the referenced verses. Ask them to request the Lord to make the subject of each paragraph reality in their personal life.

Follow through on other disciplines. Check the outlines from sermons, prayer requests, Bible study notes, and Scripture memory.

222: THE MASTER'S PLAN
Session 13

RESTITUTION FOR SIN

Assignment for Session 12:
   a. Complete: Questions for *Restitution for Sin*
   b. Memorize: Matthew 5:24
   c. Conduct: Daily Devotions
   d. Take: Sermon Notes

Introductory Summary: Believers must understand what the Bible teaches about restitution. This is a much neglected subject. It is a grievous doctrine because it strips away defensive mechanisms in our personality, and requires that we face ourselves. The principle is Biblical and should be practiced if one desires to walk the spirit-anointed way.

Questions:

1. Use a good English dictionary and record the definition for restitution.

2. In the following space, record the meaning of the word "restitution" as used in Exodus 22:1-16. Explain!

3. If a man stole a sheep he was required to make restitution by giving four for every one stolen. T or F

4. When a man allowed his beast to eat in another man's field, he was responsible for making good the loss by giving his best fields and vineyards. T or F

5. If a person were responsible for a fire that consumed a man's goods, restitution was to be made (in this sense it seems that value for value is required). T or F

6. Zacchaeus proved his faith, after he was converted, by the act of restitution (Luke 19:8). T or F

7. Using Matthew 5:24 as the basis of your understanding, state how the principle of restitution is applied toward a wronged or offended brother.

NOTE: The New Testament application of restitution appears to be based on grace. The Old Testament application of restitution appears to be based on law. God did not give a legal command in The New Testament as He did in the Old, but rather He established a principle of restitution.

Restitution benefits:
1. It cleanses one's conscience. (Through restitution, the believer gains a clear conscience and is not hindered in God's service. If a believer has sin in his life, Satan can use it as a handle to hold him back.)
2. It is a testimony to the grace of God at work in your life.
3. It offers proof that you are genuine in repentance.

Your mentor will discuss with you the following guidelines for making restitution:
1. Make sure God is directing your restitution.
2. Make sure your motive is pure.
3. Be careful not to make excuses when convicted to make restitution.
4. Do not involve others who may have been guilty.

NOTES

MENTOR'S GUIDE—SESSION 13
RESTITUTION FOR SIN

Restitution has seemingly become a forgotten concept. Few pulpits remind their hearers that God wants wrong corrected. God expects His children to act righteously. You now have an opportunity to remind yourself and your disciple that God wants His people to practice righteous living. A responsible part of right-living is making right those wrongs that have caused others to suffer loss because of our action.

There is a real danger when considering such subjects as restitution. For example, one can easily fall into the trap of legalism by applying the principle in a slavish manner. God's forgiveness is not based on our making restitution. Our acceptance is based on grace. Grace forgives as we confess and repent. But where possible, we are to right our wrongs.

Restitution is the proof of divine grace operating in ones life.

1. Check your disciple's recorded statement—make sure the proper definition was given.

2. Look for restitution being seen as compensation received for wrong suffered.

3. True (Why? Because this truth illustrates the proper compensation to a person who has been robbed.)

4. True (Take note of the extreme penalty for purposely abusing someone else's property.)

5. True (It here appears that the penalty is no more than a simple restoration of value. Why? Because, the damage was not done with an intent to defraud.)

6. True (Zacchaeus had given no previous evidence of having been interested in righting his wrongs. After his encounter with Jesus, Zacchaeus immediately became interested in righting his wrongs.)

7. The instructions here direct us to mend our fences with those we have wronged before trying to continue in our worship.

Consider carefully the notes at the end of the session. The NT principle of restitution is applied in grace. Therefore, if the wronged party is satisfied with the manner of restitution, it appears that God is satisfied. (The principle in the NT seems to be based on grace instead of preset law as in the OT.)

Cover the benefits of making restitution and try to settle any questions that may arise. When making restitution, one must be cautious. Go over the four cautions and seek to discern his degree of understanding. Correct any misunderstandings you observe. However, avoid being dogmatic because there are some debatable things about this subject. Coach your disciple to pray for spiritual guidance. Lead him to seek God's mind on this issue and to be at one with his conscience.

SUPPLEMENTAL MATERIAL & ASSIGNMENT:
Check on all assignments from last week—be sure your disciple keeps up with these disciplines. Watch for signs of growth. Remember those who are saved demonstrate the reality of God's presence as the Holy Spirit produces His fruit in them.

Ask the Father to help you discern how you may best assist in the disciple's growth. Under no conditions are you to presume to know whether another is saved. However, it is also imperative that you give no encouragement to those who claim to be saved but are living in open sin—such as drunkenness or sexual immorality. Believers are not to judge another's salvation, but we may be suspicious if there is no obvious fruit of the Spirit in their lives (Galatians 5:22, 23).

Make the next session assignments and have a season of prayer together.

NOTES

222: THE MASTER'S PLAN
Session 14

BIBLICAL FAITH

Assignment:
  a. Complete: Questions for *Biblical Faith*
  b. Memorize: Hebrews 11:1
  c. Conduct: Daily Devotions
  d. Take: Sermon Notes
  e. Study: *Faithful Is He* page 157

Introductory Summary: Faith is a fundamental concept for Christian living. It is at the very core of the Christian life and is the one ingredient, above all others, that Christ recognized as a paramount virtue. Dr. William Evans reminds us in his book on doctrine that faith is the foundation of Peter's spiritual temple (2 Peter 1:5-7), and first in Paul's trinity of graces (1Corinthians 13:13). In faith, all other graces find their effectiveness.

Questions:

1. The clearest Biblical definition for faith is found in Hebrews 11:1. (Read it carefully and record the two elements included in the definition.)

2.   Faith is commanded of the Christian (Mark 11:22; 1 John 3:23). T or F

3.   Following, is a list of Scripture references. Read the Scripture and record the object of the faith described in the reference.

SOURCE   OBJECT OF FAITH

   a.   John 14:1

   b.   John 6:29

   c.   John 5:46

   d.   2 Chronicles. 20:20

   e.   Romans 4:21

4.   Faith in Christ is:
   a.   The _____ of God
        (Romans 12:3, Ephesians 2:8, Ephesians 6:23,24, Philippians 1:29).
   b.   The _____ of God
        (Acts 11;21, I Corinthians 2:5).
   c.   Described as _____
        (II Peter 1:1).
   d.   Described as most_____
        (Jude 20).
   e.   Described as _____
        (I Thessalonians 1:3).

    f. Accompanied by_____
       (Mark 1:15, Luke 24:47).

5. Christ is the _____ and _____
(Hebrews 12:2).

6. Faith is the gift of the _____ _____
(I Corinthians 12:9).

7. The Scriptures are designed to strengthen faith (John 20:31, II Timothy 3:14, 15). T or F

8. Preaching is designed to produce faith (Acts 8:12, Romans 10:14ff, I Corinthians 3:5). T or F

9. It is impossible to _____God without faith (Hebrews 11:6).

10. Read Hebrews Chapter 11. Be prepared to discuss those who were used as illustrations of faith and the point the writer is emphasizing concerning each person. List the name first and then, the way they each showed their faith.

    NAME   HOW THEY SHOWED FAITH

    1.

    2.

    3.

    4.

5.

6.

7.

8.

9.

10.

11.

(Author Unknown)

FAITHFUL IS HE WHO CALLETH ME WHO WILL ALSO DO IT
(I THESSALONIANS 5:24)

O GOD, I CANNOT - YOU NEVER SAID I COULD.
YOU CAN - YOU ALWAYS SAID YOU WOULD
HEBREWS 10:13

I CAN DO ALL THINGS THROUGH CHRIST WHO STRENGTHENS ME.
(PHILLIPIANS 4:13)

OUR UNITY WITH THE LORD JESUS AND IT'S MEANING TO US
GALATIANS 2:20; ROMANS 6:8; 2 TIMOTHY 2:11

NOTE: THE OUTLINES ON THE FOLLOWING PAGES CONCERN OUR POSITION AND PRIVILEGES IN OUR UNION WITH CHRIST.

WE ARE UNITED IN HIS DEATH
ROMANS 6:3,5; GALATIANS 2:20

UNITY IN CHRIIT IS THE KEY TO DELIVERANCE

I. DELIVERANCE FROM THE OPPOSING FORCES OF:

- **SIN-**
  "... CONSIDER YOURSELVES TO BE DEAD TO SIN, BUT ALIVE TO GOD IN CHRIST JESUS. (ROMANS 6:6)
- **SELF-**
  FOR IF WE HAVE BECOME UNITED WITH HIM IN THE LIKENESS OF HIS DEATH,CERTAINLY WE SHALL BE ALSO IN THE LIKENESS OF HIS RESURRECTION, KNOWING THIS THAT OUR OLD SELF WAS CRUCIFIED WITH HIM, THAT OUR BODY OF SIN MIGHT BE DONE AWAY WITH THAT WE SHOULD NO LONGER BE SLAVES TO SIN. (ROMANS 6:11)
- **LAW-**
  THEREFORE, MY BRETHREN, YOU ALSO WERE MADE TO DIE TO THE LAW THROUGH THE BODY OF CHRIST, THAT YOU MIGHT BE JOINED TO ANOTHER, TO HIM WHO WAS RAISED FROM THE DEAD, THAT WE MIGHT BEAR FRUIT FOR GOD. (ROMANS 7:4)
- **WORLD-**
  BUT MAY IT NEVER BE THAT I SHOULD BOAST, EXCEPT IN THE CROSS OF OUR LORD JESUS CHRIST,
  THROUGH WHICH THE WORLD HAS BEEN CRUCIFIED TO ME, AND I TO THE WORLD. (GALATIANS 6:14)
- **SATAN-**
  THE SON OF GOD APPEARED FOR THIS PURPOSE THAT HE MIGHT DESTROY THE WORKS OF THE DEVIL. (I JOHN 3:8)

II. DELIVERANCE FROM THE OPPOSING FACTORS OF:

- **A SENSE OF CONDEMNATION:**
  THERE IS THEREFORE NOW NO CONDEMNATION FOR THOSE WHO ARE IN CHRIST JESUS. (ROMANS 8:1)
- **A SENSE OF SEPARATION:**
  WHO SHALL SEPARATE US FROM THE LOVE OF CHRIST? (ROMANS 8:35)
- **A SENSE OF INADEQUACY:**
  IN ALL THESE THINGS WE OVERWHELMINGLY CONQUER THROUGH HIM WHO LOVED US. (ROMANS 8:37)
- **A SENSE OF FEAR:**
  FOR GOD HAS NOT GIVEN US A SPIRIT OF TIMIDITY, BUT OF POWER AND LOVE AND DISCIPLINE. (2 TIMOTHY 1:7) WHEN HE HAD DISARMED THE RULERS AND AUTHORI-TIES, HE MADE A PUBLIC DISPLAY OF THEM, HAVING TRI-

UMPHED OVER THEM THROUGH HIM. (COLOSSIANS 2:15) SINCE THEN THE CHILDREN SHARE IN FLESH AND BLOOD, HE HIMSELF LIKEWISE ALSO PARTOOK OF THE SAME, THAT THROUGH DEATH HE MIGHT RENDER POWERLESS HIM WHO HAD THE POWER OF DEATH, THAT IS, THE DEVIL; AND MIGHT DELIVER THOSE WHO THROUGH FEAR OF DEATH WERE SUBJECT TO SLAVERY ALL THEIR LIVES. (HEBREWS 2:14-15)

COLOSSIANS 1:27; 2:10

WE ARE UNITED IN HIS RESURRECTION

EPHESIANS 2:6; ROMANS 6:4

THE KEYS TO HOLINESS

I. THE INDWELLING HOLY SPIRIT PRODUCES HIS FRUIT

BUT THE FRUIT OF THE SPIRIT IS: LOVE, JOY, PEACE, PATIENCE, KINDNESS, GOODNESS, FAITHFULNESS, GENTLENESS, SELF-CONTROL; AGAINST SUCH THINGS THERE IS NO LAW.

(GALATIANS 5:22)

II. THE PROMISES OF GOD

HIS DIVINE POWER HAS GRANTED TO US EVERYTHING PERTAINING TO LIFE AND GODLINESS THROUGH THE TRUE KNOWLEDGE OF HIM WHO CALLED US BY HIS OWN GLORY AND EXCELLENCE. FOR BY THESE HE HAS GRANTED TO US HIS PRECIOUS AND MAGNIFICENT PROMISES, IN ORDER THAT BY THEM YOU MIGHT BECOME PARTAKERS OF THE DIVINE NATURE, HAVING ESCAPED THE CORRUPTION THAT IS IN THE WORLD BY LUST.

2 PETER 1:3,4

AS OBEDIENT CHILDREN, DO NOT BE CONFORMED TO THE FORMER LUSTS WHICH WERE YOURS IN YOUR IGNORANCE, BUT LIKE THE HOLY ONE WHO CALLED YOU, BE HOLY YOURSELVES ALSO IN ALL YOUR BEHAVIOR; BECAUSE IT IS WRITTEN, "YOU SHALL BE HOLY, FOR I AM HOLY."

(1 PETER 1:14-16)

THEREFORE HAVING THESE PROMISES, BELOVED, LET US CLEANSE OURSELVES FROM ALL DEFILEMENT OF FLESH AND SPIRIT, PERFECTING HOLINESS IN THE FEAR OF GOD.

(2 CORINTHIANS 7:1)

ROMANS 5:17; 8:37; 1 CORINTHIANS 15:57
WE ARE UNITED IN HIS REIGN

EPHESIANS 2:6; REVELATION 1:6
THE KEYS TO VICTORIOUS SERVICE:

I. OUR SPIRITUAL POSITION
KINGS (THE RIGHT TO RULE)
- BY HIS DOING YOU ARE IN CHRIST JESUS. (1 CORINTHIANS 1:30)...WHO IS THE BLESSED SOVEREIGN, THE KING OF KINGS AND LORD OF LORDS. (1 TIMOTHY 6:15)
- MUCH MORE THOSE WHO RECEIVE THE ABUNDANCE OF GRACE AND OF THE GIFT OF RIGHTEOUSNESS WILL REIGN IN LIFE THROUGH THE ONE JESUS CHRIST. (ROMANS 5:17)

PRIESTS (THE RIGHT TO INTERCEDE)
- BUT YOU ARE A CHOSEN RACE, A ROYAL PRIESTHOOD. (I PETER 2:9)

SOLDERS (THE RIGHT TO WAR)
- SUFFER HARDSHIP WITH ME, AS A GOOD SOLDIER OF CHRIST JESUS. NO SOLDIER IN ACTIVE SERVICE ENTANGLES HIMSELF IN THE AFFAIRS OF EVERYDAY LIFE, SO THAT HE MAY PLEASE THE ONE WHO ENLISTED HIM AS A SOLDIER. (2 TIMOTHY 2:3,4)
- FOR THOUGH WE WALK IN THE FLESH, WE DO NOT WAR ACCORDING TO THE FLESH, FOR THE WEAPONS OF OUR WARFARE ARE NOT OF THE FLESH, BUT DIVINELY POWERFUL FOR THE DESTRUCTION OF FORTRESSES. WE ARE DESTROYERS OF FORTRESSES. WE ARE DESTROYERS OF SPECULATIONS AND EVERY LOFTY THING RAISED UP AGAINST THE KNOWLEDGE OF GOD, AND WE ARE TAKING EVERY THOUGHT CAPTIVE TO THE OBEDIENCE OF CHRIST. (2 CORINTHIANS 10:3-5)
- PUT ON THE FULL ARMOR OF GOD, THAT YOU MAY BE ABLE TO STAND FIRM AGAINST THE SCHEMES OF THE DEVIL. (EPHESIANS 6:11)

II. OUR SPIRITUAL ABILITY-
ABILITY RESTS UPON GOD'S PROMISES

- TRULY I SAY TO YOU, WHATEVER YOU SHALL BIND ON EARTH SHALL HAVE BEEN BOUND IN HEAVEN, AND WHATEVER YOU LOOSE ON EARTH SHALL HAVE BEEN LOOSED IN HEAVEN. AGAIN I SAY TO YOU, THAT IF TWO OF YOU AGREE ON EARTH ABOUT ANYTHING THAT THEY MAY ASK, IT SHALL BE DONE FOR THEM BY MY FATHER WHO IS IN HEAVEN. FOR WHERE TWO OR THREE HAVE GATHERED TOGETHER IN MY NAME, THERE I AM IN THEIR (MATTHEW 18:18-20)
- FOR AS MANY AS MAY BE THE PROMISES OF GOD, IN HIM THEY ARE YES; WHEREFORE ALSO BY HIM IS OUR AMEN TO THE GLORY OF GOD THROUGH US. (2 CORINTHIANS 1:20)

ABILITY IS SUPPLIED BY GOD'S GIFTS
(THE GIFTS OF THE HOLY SPIRIT)

- AND SINCE WE HAVE GIFTS THAT DIFFER ACCORDING TO THE GRACE GIVEN TO US LET EACH EXERCISE THEM ACCORDINGLY. (ROMANS 12:6)
- NOW THERE ARE VARIETIES OF GIFTS, BUT THE SAME SPIRIT. (I CORINTHIANS 12:4)
- AS EACH ONE HAS RECEIVED A SPECIAL GIFT, EMPLOY IT IN SERVING ONE ANOTHER, AS GOOD STEWARDS OF THE MANIFOLD GRACE OF GOD. (I PETER 4:10)
- WHATEVER YOU DO, DO YOUR WORK HEARTILY, AS FOR THE LORD RATHER THAN FOR MEN, KNOWING THAT FROM THE LORD YOU WILL RECEIVE THE REWARD OF THE INHERITANCE. IT IS THE LORD CHRIST WHOM YOU SERVE. (COLOSSIANS 3:23,24)
- FOR IN HIM ALL THE FULLNESS OF DEITY DWELLS IN BODILY FORM, AND IN HIM YOU HAVE BEEN MADE COMPLETE, AND HE IS THE HEAD OVER ALL RULE AND AUTHORITY... COLOSSIANS 2:9-10
- ABIDE IN ME, AND I IN YOU...THAT YOUR JOY MAY BE FULL. (JOHN 15:4,11)

161

PROCLAMATION OF FAITH

I BELIEVE IN THE SON OF GOD

THEREFORE,

I AM IN HIM,
HAVING REDEMPTION THROUGH HIS BLOOD,
AND LIFE BY HIS SPIRIT,

HE IS IN ME, AND
ALL FULLNESS IS IN HIM.

TO HIM I BELONG BY —
CREATION—PURCHASE—CONQUEST
& SELF-SURRENDER

TO ME HE BELONGS FOR ALL MY HOURLY NEEDS.
THERE IS NO CLOUD BETWEEN MY LORD AND
ME.

THERE IS NO DIFFICULTY INWARD
OR OUTWARD WHICH
HE IS NOT READY TO MEET IN ME TODAY.

I BELIEVE - I HAVE RECEIVED,
NOT THE SPIRIT OF FEAR,
BUT OF POWER
AND OF LOVE
AND OF A SOUND MIND.
THE LORD IS MY KEEPER

Mentor's Guide - Session 14
Biblical Faith

We open with a statement regarding the importance of faith and how essential it is to the Christian. One word of caution should be heard and understood: "Faith in faith is worthless." Biblical faith has an object! Saving faith is directed to God! It is dependent on God's promise of forgiveness. Because Christ died for those who believe on Him. Plant the previous statement in the soil of your disciple's heart and water it often. Why? We live in a culture given to sentimentalism that often produces false hope because of misdirected faith.

1. The two elements of faith you are seeking are "substance" and "evidence." (Explain that faith must have these two elements for hope of fulfillment. Substance is reality. Faith is belief that the thing in which one places his confidence is real. Evidence is information that provides rational support for placing faith in a thing or person.)

2. True. (God has given the believer faith as a gift, and he is expected to exercise it.)

3. The following should be reflected in your disciple's record:

    a. John 14:1   Christ
    b. John 6:29   Christ
    c. John 5:46   Word

    d. 2 Chronicles 20:20   Lord
    f. Romans 4:21   Word (Promises)

4. Faith in Christ is: (The blanks are filled as follows:)
    a. Grace
    b. Power
    c. Righteousness
    d. Holy
    e. Work
    f. Repentance

5. The blanks should be filled with the words "author" and "finisher." These words indicate the eternal character of Christ's person.

6. The "Holy Spirit" is the giver of faith. Be certain this fact registers with your disciple. (Biblical or saving faith is not the natural possession of the lost person. Therefore, you cannot exercise what you do not have.)

7. True! God's Word produces faith in the heart of the believer.

8. True! Preaching by God's anointed messenger is designed to strengthen the faith of the hearer. Only believers will have ears to hear the message of God and those whose spiritual eyes and ears are opened by the Holy Spirit.

9. The key word here is "please." The faith of the believing heart is precious in the sight of God. The heart of unbelief will never please Him.

10. You will need to do your homework here. Take a concordance and look up the names of those listed as examples in Hebrews chapter eleven. Choose some of the characters cited for discussion in your session.

SUPPLEMENTAL MATERIAL & ASSIGNMENT :
While the questions for this lesson have been rather brief and simple, do not think the subject unimportant. Biblical Faith may well be the centerpiece of man's experience in Biblical Christianity.

The disciple must be taught the importance of relating to God on the basis of faith in Christ. Spend the necessary time to ensure a thorough understanding of "saving" faith. I recommend a book on the subject by A. W. Pink.

Check your assignment sheet assuring that all responsibilities have been satisfied. (I must continue to alert you to the importance of not letting the disciple get by without doing the assignments. Why? When assignments are missed, the process appears casual and unimportant. I can testify concerning the damaging affect of taking shortcuts. You are molding a life through this process. Cutting corners will only undermine the discipline your purpose to build into his or her life.)

As a mentor, you are God's agent in the disciple's life and are even being used to refine a precious gem to the glory of God.

Go over the article on faith and have your disciple share its truth in his own words. If you feel that greater understanding is needed, you may suggest the article be studied again during next week's devotional time. Call special attention to how our faith in Christ has given us victory.

Through faith in His dying for our sins, we are united to Him. Our union with Christ has three specific results:
    (1) Our union results in deliverance from the judgement of sin.
    (2) Our union results in deliverance from the present power of sin.
    (3) Our union results in victory over the tyranny of sin as He lives His life through us.

Make the applicable assignments and have a time of personal prayer.

222: THE MASTER'S PLAN
Session 15

TRANSFORMING THE MIND

Assignment:
   a. Complete: Questions for Transforming the Mind
   b. Memorize: Philippians 2:5
   c. Conduct: Daily Devotions
   d. Take: Sermon Notes
   e. Study: the Chart: *How Man Functions* page 171

Introductory Summary: As a basis for our thinking together, read—Ephesians 4:23, Matthew 15:19, and
Proverbs 23:7. When God has control of one's mind, He
controls the body as well. So, the Christian must be diligent
about thinking God's thoughts. The following questions
will emphasize the thought life. We will consider the mind
and the transformation that brings glory to God.

Questions:

1. In Romans 1:28, God refers to the natural mind as a
_____ mind (the mind of one who is unconverted
which is in rebellion against God).

2. In 2 Corinthians 3:14, the natural mind, which is cor-
rupt and cannot receive spiritual Truth, is described as
_____.

3. In Genesis 13:5-13, the _____ are examples of those who have a natural mind (a mind which is bathed in darkness and cannot receive spiritual Truth). (The Pharisees in the Gospels are illustrations of men who have blinded spiritual minds).

4. Two types of minds exist among Christians. The carnal, or fleshly oriented mind operates on a low spiritual plain. In Genesis 13:5-12 we see _____ , Abraham's nephew, as an illustration of one who has a carnal mind.

5. Lot was a just man, a righteous man, but _____ himself with his wicked surroundings. (II Peter 2:6-9)

6. In accordance with I John 2:15, it appears that Lot was a man who was concerned with the things of the _____.

7. The carnal mind is the antithesis of the Spiritual mind when viewed from within Christianity. Those who have a spiritual orientation are those who live on a high spiritual plain. In Genesis13:5-12 we see another person recorded. He is one who is an example of the spiritually minded man. His name is _____ .

(He walked after the spirit of God. He specialized in the things of God rather than the things of the world. Note: He was not without fault, but he continually aspired after God's holiness.)

8. The transformation of the mind is appropriated by faith. One must believe Christ will influence his mind for the sake of God's right purpose when he submits to Christ as Lord (Philippians 2:5, I Corinthians 2:14-16). T or F

9. God will _____ the mind with His Word (Jeremiah 15:16).

10. God will _____ the mind, which is committed to Him (Philippians 4:7).

11. God will keep _____ that heart or mind that is stayed upon Him (Psalm 139:23-24).

12. The mind is transformed through the application of 2 Corinthians 10:4, 5. Read these verses and be prepared to discuss the steps required to move from a carnal to a spiritual state. (Record your notes below.)

NOTES

HOW MAN FUNCTIONS

THROUGH HIS SENSES MAN RECEIVES INFORMATION FROM THE PHYSICAL WORLD AROUND HIM.

THROUGH THE SPIRIT MAN RECEIVES INFORMATION FROM GOD AND SPIRITUAL BEINGS (THE TWO POLES IN THE SPIRIT CIRCLE REPRESENT THE INPUT FROM GOOD & EVIL ANGELS)

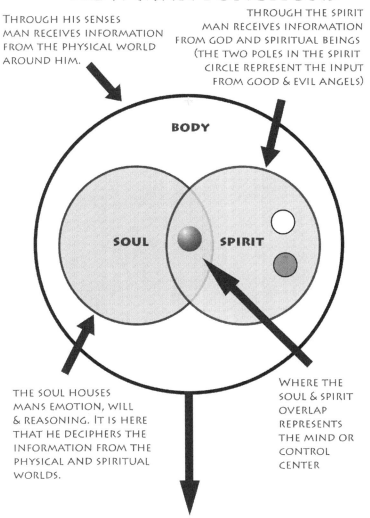

THE SOUL HOUSES MANS EMOTION, WILL & REASONING. IT IS HERE THAT HE DECIPHERS THE INFORMATION FROM THE PHYSICAL AND SPIRITUAL WORLDS.

WHERE THE SOUL & SPIRIT OVERLAP REPRESENTS THE MIND OR CONTROL CENTER

ACTION IS TAKEN BY THE BODY WHEN MAN DECIDES TO EXERCISE HIS WILL BASED ON THE INFORMATION HE RECEIVES FROM THE PHYSICAL AND SPIRITUALS INPUTS.

Design by: W. L. Owens

THREE CLASSES OF MEN

THE NATURAL MAN
THE NATURAL MAN IS
LOST. HE IS DEAD TO
SPIRITUAL THINGS. THE
SHADED POLE INDICATES
HIS DEADNESS TO GOD.

THE CARNAL MAN:
THE CARNAL MAN IS A
CHRISTIAN WHOSE LIFE IS
CO-EXISTING WITH KNOWN
SIN. THUS THE POSITIVE
CIRCLES IS SHADED & THE
NEGATIVE CIRCLE IS CLEAR.

THE SPIRITUAL MAN
THE SPIRITUAL MAN IS ONE
WHO HAS NO KNOWN SIN
CLOUDING HIS FELLOWSHIP
WITH GOD. THEREFORE, THE
POSITIVE POLE IS CLEAR.

NOTE: IN EACH OF THE ILLUSTRATIONS THERE IS BOTH A POSITIVE
AND NEGATIVE POLE IN THE SPIRIT CIRCLE. THE UPPER SPIRIT CIRCLE
REPRESENTS COMMUNICATION FROM GOD AND ANGELS. THE LOWER
CIRCLE INDICATES INFORMATION FROM SATAN & DEMONS. A SHADED
CIRCLE INDICATES HINDERED TRANSMISSION OF INFORMATION.

Design by: W. L. Owens

Mentor's Guide— Session 15
Transforming the Mind

The Christian's ultimate goal is to become like Christ. Christ likeness is never more realized than when one's motive is to fulfill the mind of Christ. Paul in writing to the Philippians exhorted them, "Let this mind (or manner of thinking) be in you which was also in Christ Jesus." (Phil. 2:5) Whatever may be said about the mind of Christ, one may be sure its primary purpose is obedience to God.

In the following questions and charts you will lead the disciple to discover how important it is to possess a transformed mind. God will "guard" the mind that is committed to Him. (He guards the mind through His Truth. Therefore, the primary reference is to let Truth be the "guardian.")

1. The blank for question one should be "debased" or possibly "reprobate."

2. The "natural" mind is also described as a "hardened" mind.

3. The Canaanites and Sodomites are examples of those who have "natural" minds.

4. Lot is an illustration of how a Christian who is "carnally" minded, might act. (The carnal Christian's activity is governed by the wisdom of the flesh not the wisdom of God.)

5. Lot was a righteous man. However, his "carnal" activity placed him in situations that vexed his soul. (II Pet. 2:7, 8)

6. Unfortunately, Christians sometimes lose their sense of direction or their moral compass is affected by the flesh and like Lot, appear to be in love with the things of the "world."

7. "Abraham," when contrasted with Lot, is seen to be a man who majored in spiritual wisdom. He was a man whose life was also marred by sin, but Abraham was different from Lot in the motivation of his heart.

8. "True." All the graces of God are received by faith; i.e., simply believing God to keep His promise.

9. God will "renew" the mind with His Word. (Lead your disciple to see that the Word of God is the primary instrument our Father uses in bring about change.)

10. God will "guard" the mind that is committed to Him. (Lead your disciple to see that our commitment to God is a commitment to His Word.)

11. The Lord will keep "pure" the heart that is stayed on Him. (When a believer focuses on God and His holiness, he begins to "become" what he sees.)

12. Moving from a carnal to a spiritual state is like changing the oil in your spiritual engine. The steps that lead to change are:
    a. Identify the hindering sin by focusing on God's viewpoint. (Philippians 2:5)

b. Take your position with God against your sin and repent. (James 4:7,8)

c. Receive God's forgiveness by faith in His promise (I John 1:8,9).

d. Obedience, is the focus of your love for Him. (John 14:15)

SUPPLEMENTAL MATERIAL & ASSIGNMENT:

The diagrams on pages 171 & 172, will greatly aid the disciple in understanding how behavioral changes are accomplished. All men and women are subject to change. All change comes through the transformation of the mind. The mind is transformed by its focus. The psalmist wrote: "...as a man thinketh in his heart, so is he." This truth moved Tim Lahaye to write *Battle for the Mind.* Why? Because if Satan or his fallen angels can gain an advantage in our minds, it will largely determine our attitude and actions.

Request the disciple, to read over the chart titled *How Man Functions.* Study the article *Explanation of How Man Functions* on page 177; be prepared to share with your disciple its unique structure.

NOTES

EXPLANATION OF
HOW MAN FUNCTIONS

The large circle represents man's physical body. (Through the body's physical senses, information is gathered from the physical world for making life decisions and taking action.)

The two smaller circles represent the invisible parts of man and are designated as "soul" and "spirit." (These are shown to overlap because we cannot discern precisely where one begins and the other ends. Scholars have debated for centuries over whether man is made of two parts or three. Our purposes will not be served by entering that argument. Therefore, consider the circles as an illustration of the functions of man and not his parts.)

(1.) The circle marked "spirit" serves as our link to the spirit or supernatural world. It is through our spirit that both God and His angels communicate with our spirit. As the body receives information from the physical world, the spirit assimilates impulses and spiritual impressions from the unseen reality of a supernatural world. (Satan and demons, as fallen angels can also communicate with us through our spirit.)

(2.) The circle marked "mind" represents the part of us that functions as a control center like the central processing unit of a personal computer. Our mind deciphers the information received from the physical and the spiritual worlds. Based upon the relevant information, the individual determines a course of action based upon the exercise of his own will. God has granted man the ability to make choices through this evaluation process. Therefore, our bodies act because of the information received and the options perceived. Knowing this process may be the reason Jesus said it's not what goes in a man's belly that defiles him, but what comes out of his heart. (Matthew 15:18-20)

These three circles relating to one another illustrate how man functions or how he makes his decisions about the issues of life. Lead your disciple to an understanding of the above process before going to the chart.

Look for the chart titled— *Three Classes of Man*—it is provided to illustrate the current state of mankind. Everyone now living may be classified by one of the three illustrations on the chart.

The Natural Man - Note that the same three circles described above are in each of the graphics. Also, note that there is either one or two other circles in each graphic. These smaller circles are located within the larger circle marked "spirit" and represent one of two spiritual sources. The small darkened circle represents satanic and demonic influence upon the individual. Prior to salvation the individual is dead to God and is only receiving spiritual information from Satan and his fallen angels.

The Carnal Man - As in the previous graphic, you will notice the smaller circles within the larger one marked "spirit." In this graphic, there is a darkened and a shaded circle. The graphic reflects what happens in the life of one who knows God but is not walking in the light of God's council. Both Satan and God have access to the believer. When the believer chooses to disobey the Lord, the clear circle is shaded indicating he is not following God's direction and is therefore giving preference to Satan. The condition described above is known as backsliding. The only remedy is found in I John 1:7-9. When the disciple obeys John's admonition, fellowship with God is restored.

The Spiritual Man - The "spirit" circle has a smaller darkened circle indicating the access Satan and his emissaries have to the believer's life. More important, there is a small clear circle showing the believer to be actively obedient to the Master. Active, moment by moment, obedience is what qualifies one for the classification of "spiritual."

Lead your disciple to a clear understanding of the above concepts. However, remember that graphic representation of spiritual truth is usually flawed in some point. Illustrations, graphic or otherwise, are only representations of truth and not truth in essence.

NOTES

222: THE MASTER'S PLAN
SESSION 16

THE CHRISTIAN
AND SUFFERING

Assignment:
   a. Complete: Questions for *Christian & Suffering*
   b. Memorize: II Timothy 3:12
   c. Conduct: Daily Devotions
   d. Take: Sermon Notes

Introductory Summary: Carefully read I Peter 1:3-9. Peter has here presented the sovereignty of God within the context of salvation. Now, the Apostle focuses upon how God brings believers to completeness through daily spiritual living. Our passage may be divided into two parts: the first (vs. 3-5) is a continuation of the theme dealing with salvation; the second (vs. 6-9) deals with the explanation of why Christian suffering is important and necessary.

Questions:

1. Reread I Peter 1: 6 and explain why suffering is not permanent. (Note the phrase: "… for a season.")

2. In the same verse you find the phrase: "… if need be." Explain why suffering is always significant. (Include in your consideration Romans 8:28, 29.)

3. The believer becomes effective in Christian service through suffering. As gold is refined through the jewelers fire, so the Christian's faith is refined through trials and suffering. (Malachi 3:3; I Peter 1:6-9) T or F

4. Suffering comes through every part of one's being. As you reflect on your last study, cite the three parts of man that are subject to suffering.

5. Read again the passage cited above (I Peter 1:6-9). Record from verse seven what you perceive to be the central purpose for Christian suffering.

6. One is disciplined and spiritually educated through suffering (Hebrews 5:8, 12:7, 8). T or F

7. Suffering teaches us to be humble (II Corinthians 12:7, Deuteronomy 8:2,3). T or F

8. Suffering qualifies us to help others (II Corinthians1:3-7). T or F

9. Suffering gives us a hunger or longing for heaven (Philippians 1:23). T or F

Suffering is a vital ingredient in maintaining spiritual power. God does not cause suffering, but it is one of the tools He uses in fashioning us to become like Jesus Christ. (Romans 8:28, 29) The book of Job records the classic example of the ministry of suffering.

NOTES

Mentor's Guide—Session 16
The Christian & Suffering

Suffering is a vital part of God's program of spiritual growth. The mature disciple will learn to praise God even in the midst of suffering. We must learn to trust our Lord. He will never allow suffering to hinder our spiritual growth.

Discuss the subject of suffering and discern where your disciple is in his or her understanding. Use each of the questions in this lesson as a discussion starter for deepening the appreciation for suffering in life.

1.   The phrase "... for a season," is the key to our understanding. Suffering will not last forever. It will end at some point in this life or God will cause it to end with our death.

2.   The disciple should discern from I Peter 1:6 that every event in the Christian's life is in some way directed or allowed by the Lord. Even our mistakes and acts of open rebellion that cause God pain will be used of Him to bring glory to His name. One should be careful not to lead others to think that God endorses sin. Quite the contrary! However, He does allow suffering and will cause it to work for our good and His glory. Only God can make circumstances work together for good.

3.   It is true. Suffering is like an instrument of refinement in the Lord's hand. It is much like the jeweler whose fire is an aid in the purifying of precious metals.

4. Man is the subject of suffering in all three aspects of his being. He suffers physically through diseases and accidents. He suffers spiritually from spiritual warfare with Satan and his fallen angels. Mentally, we suffer through the emotional extremes caused either by the circumstances of life or by our unwillingness to trust God's deliverance. If your disciple does not agree with the above concepts, ask him to provide a Biblical reason for objecting.

5. The central purpose for Christian suffering is the purifying of our faith in God as the Lord of our lives.

6. Chastening through suffering is a strategy employed by our loving Father to make us into the likeness of His Son— our Savior. (Jesus learned through suffering, but in His case the suffering did not come a result of sin or as chastisement. He never sinned nor deviated from His Father's plan for His life.)

7. Humility comes when we are made to see that our natural efforts have no power to change the cause of our suffering. If we could, we would. Like Job, we are privileged to present our lives to God and thank Him for the grace to bear our suffering to His glory.

8. Personal suffering equips one to aid other souls who pass through the deep waters of trouble. It behooves us to learn through suffering. Why? Because, we want God to receive glory, when out of our suffering, we minister to others.

9. Physical suffering wearies the human body, and becomes one means God uses to prepare us for heaven.

SUPPLEMENTAL MATERIAL & ASSIGNMENTS:

Discuss thoroughly, the subject of suffering with your disciple. Do not proceed until you are satisfied he understands how suffering is used of God in our life. Christians must understand that God has not promised us wealth, health, and happiness. He knows that a realization of His holiness is far more satisfying than mere human happiness. What He has promised is abundant life. If our Lord was subjected to suffering in this world, then we should not expect to escape it.

Be sure to hold the disciple responsible for his sermon notes, memory verses, and other disciplines that are so necessary for establishing a good foundation. However, remember these lessons and disciplines are not our ultimate goal. Our goal is to glorify our Lord in daily living.

Worship the Lord together and share in a time of prayer before parting.

NOTES

222: THE MASTER'S PLAN
Session 17

VICTORY IN
SPIRITUAL CONFLICT

Assignment:
  a. Complete: Questions for *Spiritual Conflict*
  b. Memorize: Ephesians 6:12
  c. Conduct: Daily Devotions
  d. Take: Sermon Notes
  e. Study: *Finding Divine Guidance* page 193

Introductory Summary:

Meditatively read Ephesians 6:10-18. It is important that we maintain a spiritual stance. Having come to know Christ as Savior, we must continue to walk in Him. Satan has set himself against our daily walk with Christ. However, Satan is not the all-powerful enemy he seems to be!

He is subject to the sovereignty of Christ. There is absolutely no hope for those without Christ, but those who are redeemed have abundant provisions to withstand the wiles of the devil. Satan's ploys are no match for the well equipped believer.

The questions below will reveal the provisions our Father has made for His children to successfully engage our enemy.

Questions:

1. Read Ephesians 6:10 and record in whose strength we must abide.

2. According to Ephesians 6:11, what must we do before we try to stand against the wiles of the devil?

3. In verse twelve, Paul reveals the nature of our enemy. In your own words, describe your perception of that nature.

4. In verse 13, the Christian is exhorted to "withstand" and to "stand". Using these terms, what do you perceive Paul is asking these Ephesians to do?

5. Referring again to Ephesians 6:13, what does it mean to take unto you the whole armor of God?

6. In verses Ephesians 6:14-17, we are given a description of the armor of God. List these pieces of armor and opposite them list the spiritual defense mechanisms they represent.

Example:

    1. Girdle   Truth

    2.

    3.

    4.

    5.

    6.

7.   In Ephesians 6:16, the shield of faith is used to quench the fiery darts of the wicked. Discuss what this means to you.

8.   If the Christian's defense is to be the armor of God, what is to be the base support for that armor? You should discover two activities that are objects of Paul's exhortation. (vs. 18)

We are engaged in a spiritual warfare (Ephesians 6:17). Therefore, let us commit ourselves to intercessory prayer.

FINDING DIVINE GUIDANCE

by George Muller

I seek in the beginning to get my heart into such a state that it has no will of its own in regard to a given matter. (Nine-tenths of the trouble with people is just here. Nine-tenths of the difficulties are over our hearts not being ready to do the Lord's will, whatever it may be. When one is truly in this state, it is usually but a little way to the knowledge of what His will is.)

Having done this, I do not leave the result to feeling or simple impression. (If I do so, I make myself liable to great delusions.) I seek the will of the Spirit of God through, or in connection with, the Word of God. (The Spirit and the Word must be combined. If I look to the Spirit alone without the Word, I lay myself open to great delusions also. If the Holy Ghost guides us at all, He will do it according to the Scriptures and never contrary to them.)

Next, I take into account providential circumstances. (These often plainly indicate God's will in connection with His Word and Spirit.) I ask God in prayer to reveal His will to me.

Thus, through prayer to God, the study of the Word, and reflection, I come to a deliberate judgment according to the best of my ability and knowledge, and if my mind is thus at peace, and continues so after two or three more petitions, I proceed accordingly. In trivial matters, and in transactions involving most important issues, I have found this method always effective.

NOTES

Mentor's Guide—Session 17
Victory in Spiritual Conflict

Our present topic is most critical! All Christians, need a proper understanding of the enemy. Satan and his evil angels have set themselves against God and all who serve Him. God uses Satan to accomplish His ultimate goal of purifying all that exists. While Satan plays a major part in God's plan, he is still a major hindrance to our faithful service. Therefore, it is essential that we understand the power and limitations of our spiritual enemy.

1.   The believer must come to see that his own strength is grossly insufficient when facing his enemy. Our only hope for victory in our skirmishes with Satan is the strength of the Lord.

2.   Christians are being encouraged to put on our spiritual protection that is, the "whole armor of God."

3.   Satan is the leader of a huge number of fallen angels, these angels are organized into a structured hierarchy of principalities, powers, and rulers. There is room here for some variation of understanding. Don't be too dogmatic. The essential truth to grasp is that Satan is our real enemy who uses a myriad of fallen angels (also know as demons) to do his bidding in this world.

4.   Paul is here exhorting Christians in Ephesus to stand firm in God's strength in the face of Satan's onslaught. We may lose some of the skirmishes, but He has already won the war for us. Therefore, in faith, stand firm.

5. Note the words: "Put on the whole armor of God."
Some years ago, I remembered I had read the above phrase
(or one similar) in another place. I did some research and
discovered a passage using similar phrasing in Romans
13:12-14. At that moment, I saw clearly that putting on
Christ as Lord of one's life, and putting on the armor of
God were one and the same act. When the believer comes
to Christ as Lord, then Jesus becomes for him everything
listed in Ephesians 6. Jesus becomes our breastplate of
righteousness. He is our feet shod with the Gospel of peace.
He is our shield of faith, etc. Christ is totally the sole suffi-
ciency of the believer.

6. JESUS IS OUR ALL:

a.	Girdle	Truth	Jesus is our "TRUTH."
b.	Breastplate	Righteousness	Christ is our Righteousness.
c.	Shoes	Peace	Jesus is our peace that passes all understanding.
d.	Shield	Faith	Our "faith" in Christ quenches Satan's fiery darts.
e.	Helmet	Salvation	Jesus is our covering— protecting us with His Salvation.
f.	Sword	Spirit	Jesus is the Word and protects us by the Spirit of His Word.

7.   Lead the disciple to understand that fiery darts may re-fer to any attack launched against the believer. (The reason Satan attacks Christians is caused by of their association with Christ. It appears that Satan's hatred for God is so great that he attacks what he thinks will hurt God the most. The Scriptures call him "the accuser of the brethren." He attacks our greatest weakness. When we fall, our failure brings reproach to God's name.)

8.   The two activities in question are found in verse eigh-teen of the passage and are (1) prayer and (2) watching. (Remind those you instruct that the Christian faith is any-thing but passive. We cannot afford to be spiritually lazy. God has in His sovereignty appointed us to be co-laborers with Him.)

SUPPLEMENTAL MATERIAL & ASSIGNMENT:

Have your disciple read and meditate on the brief outline by George Mueller titled *Determining Divine Guidance*. Ask some hard questions about the article. Try to determine if he has discernment about divine leadership. You might ask how Mueller would have understood God's leadership and how he would have prepared himself to follow the Lord's lead.

COMPLETE WEEKLY DISCIPLINES:

NOTES

222: THE MASTER'S PLAN
Session 18

PERSONAL EVANGELISM I

Assignment:
 a. Study: the Lesson Outline
 b. Memorize: Romans 6:23
 c. Conduct: Daily Devotions
 d. Take: Sermon Notes
 e. Discuss: *My Testimony Outline* page 203

I. Some Fundamental Questions
 A. What is evangelism?
  Presenting the gospel to a lost person so that he may have opportunity to receive or reject God's gracious offer of salvation to "whosoever believeth" (John 3:16).
 B. Why must the gospel be presented?
  1. The Bible argues that a person cannot believe unless he hears the gospel, and he cannot hear unless someone tells him (Romans 10:13-14).
  2. The Scriptures emphatically teach that the person who believes has everlasting life, and the one who has not believed is already under God's awful condemnation (John 3:36).
 C. Who should do evangelism?
  1. Who should do public or mass evangelism?
   a. The evangelist (Ephesians 4:11-12).
   b. The Pastor and elders (II Timothy 4:5).
   c. The Deacons (Acts 8:5).

    d. The believers, who spread the good news (Acts 8:4; I Thessalonians 1:8; Mark 2:4-5).

2. Who should do Personal Evangelism - To be done by every believer.

    a. God's purpose - The Lord chooses us that we might go and bring forth fruit (John 15:16, Proverbs 11:30).

    b. God's command - Jesus commands us to take the gospel to every person in every nation in every generation (Great Comm.) (Mark 16:15; Matt. 28:18-20; Acts 1:8).

    c. God's economy - God's first command to mankind in Genesis is "to be fruitful and multiply." (Genesis 1:28)

    d. Everything should reproduce after its kind (Genesis 1:11).

        1. Dawson Trotman, founder of the Navigators, originated the counseling system used by Billy Graham and other evangelists in city-wide crusades. Mr. Trotman taught that God intends that we reproduce spiritually as well as physically.

        2. Every Christian is "Born to Reproduce."

        3. Examples:

           a. Dogs produce puppies.

           b. Cats produce kittens.

           c. Cows produce calves.

           d. _____ produce Christians.

        Quotation: "Anyone who knows enough to be saved knows enough to tell some

one else how to be saved." - Dawson
Trotman

D. Application: Are you a fruitful Christian? Has God used you to bring another soul Christ? You can be fruitful! In fact, God expects you to bear fruit to His glory. Here's how you can prepare yourself to be come a fruitful believer:

II. Keys to Personal Evangelism

A. Witness by life. (WALK)

We witness through our life including our talk. But if we are not living up to the standard expected of a Christian, others are going to be turned off to our message. They will say in their hearts, "Your acts speak so loud I cannot hear your words." How should we live as Christians? The book of Ephesians gives us instructions:

1. Walk worthily - Ephesians 4:1 We should walk worthy of our calling as a Christian, a follower of Christ's teachings. We watch our conduct so as not to be a stumbling block to unbelievers.

2. Walk lovingly - Ephesians 5:2 If we really love a person we will find ways to show this. "Love finds a way." Also, if we lack this personal concern, it will show.

3. Walk carefully (circumspectly) - Ephesians 5:15 We should avoid offending the person we are trying to reach. Put yourself in his shoes. Ob serve those prejudices that may be due to family background or culture (I Corinthians 9:19-22). Illustration:The motto of *Young Life* is: "No offense short of the offense of the cross." (We

must never compromise the Gospel regardless of how offensive it may be!)

B. Witness through friendships. (WINSOME)
1. If we want to make friends, we must show our selves friendly (Proverbs 18:24). The initiative should come from us.
2. Jesus went out of his way to identify with sinners (Luke 15:1; Luke 5:30, 31).
3. The Apostle Paul gives his testimony three times in the book of Acts. In Chapter 26 he gives us a good pattern to follow in developing one's own testimony.
   a. What my life was like before Christ (4-11).
   b. When, where, how—I came to Christ (12-18).
   c. How my life changed after Christ (19-23).
Note: In regards to your testimony, be sure not to glorify the past; glorify Christ.

MY PERSONAL TESTIMONY

Before coming to Christ my life was . . .

I saw my need for Christ when . . .

I received Christ when I . . .

Since coming to Christ my life has . . .

NOTES

Mentor's Guide— Session 18
Personal Evangelism (I)

With this lesson, we take up Christ's command to make disciples. Making disciples begins with the communication of God's message to man. Contrary to various versions of "pop theology," it is not—"smile, God loves you." God's message begins with the holiness of God and the wickedness of sinful man. Disciples are followers of Christ's way of life. One cannot follow Christ until he first knows Christ. One cannot know Christ until he first sees his absolute need for acceptance by Christ. Acceptance by Christ is not dependent on man but on the grace of God.

Because of the Father's provision in His Son, eternal life is given to those who come to Christ for mercy and forgiveness of sin. One must abandon all efforts to be accepted on the grounds of his own goodness or acts of personal righteousness. The Bible makes it quite clear that we are not accepted because of "our" performance but on God's grace alone. Communicating the above truth is our task.

(Study the outline in detail and go over the points until you are satisfied there is understanding of the concepts. These three lessons on evangelism are different, than the previous ones. Therefore, your approach is more direct than inductive. If possible, take your disciple into a witnessing environment so he may observe you practice what is being taught during these sessions. Be sure to stress the importance of relationships in evangelistic encounters.)

The lesson outline has two divisions. (Study the comments below and any other materials that will help you assist those whom you teach.)

SOME FUNDAMENTAL QUESTIONS

What is evangelism? The definition provided in the workbook is a simple non-technical answer. The Biblical answer is more accurately stated in the opening paragraph. Use the information above as your basic evangelism philosophy. Why must the gospel be presented? Study the verses in the Romans 10:13-14. Please note the word "heard." The reference is to physical hearing. One will never believe beyond his base of information. Therefore, someone must be committed to sharing the facts of the Gospel. We will deal with other aspects of hearing in a subsequent session.

Who should do evangelism? The disciple should have impressed upon his heart how essential is his own personal participation in evangelizing our world. Points 1, 2 & 3 are rather straightforward; study them carefully and engage your disciple in a discussion about both their meanings and implications.

(Please note at the conclusion of this section there is a reference to Dawson Trotman and a blank that must be filled. Complete the blank with the word "Christians.")

KEYS TO PERSONAL EVANGELISM

(From this section, you must share the need for witnesses to have a well rounded and spiritually balanced life. We must be willing to live by what we say we believe, or our message will not have credibility. The Young Life motto means that believers should avoid at all costs, anything that would be offensive to those being witnessed to. The only exception to the stated rule is the message of the Cross. If the Gospel offends, so be it.)

SUPPLEMENTAL MATERIAL & ASSIGNMENT:

The memory verses for personal evangelism are crucial to the disciple's success in bringing people to Christ. Stress a word-for-word accuracy in learning these verses. (Go over the personal testimony again. Emphasize how important it is that a witness be able to share his own personal story in about ninety-seconds. Ask him to write out his testimony using the form provided in the workbook.)

NOTES

NOTES222:THE MASTER'S PLAN
Session 19

PERSONAL EVANGELISM II

Assignment:
a. Study: the lesson outline
b. Memorize: Romans 3:23; 6:23
c. Conduct: Daily Devotions
d. Take: Sermon Notes
e. Write out your testimony using the *My Testimony Outline* (Follow the pattern of Acts 26. Make it short and specific; it should not go over two minutes when read.)

Outline:

I. The Bridge Illustration

The "Bridge" is a tool used by many believers to present the "Gospel" in graphic form. The illustration was originally developed by Roy Robertson who was a missionary to Asia. The Asian mind is graphic in its orientation. Therefore, God led Roy to use the "Bridge" as an illustration of the only way man can come to God. (The illustration included in the *222 Plan* is an adapted version of the original and has a greater emphasis on repentance.)

II. Explanation (Ask your mentor to go over the *Bridge of Life* Illustration. A description of the steps used in sharing the *Bridge of Life* is found in the *Mentor's Guide —Lesson 19.*) In evangelism, with the leading of the Holy Spirit, we create an atmosphere so that God may do His work of saving souls.

A. In order for a person to be saved the:
    1. Mind must be enlightened
    2. Emotions must be stirred
    3. Will must be changed
B. Three questions to ask after presenting *The Bridge of Life:*
    1. Do you understand it?
    2. Are you willing to believe?
    3. Will you pray now to receive by faith the Lord Jesus Christ as Lord of your life and as your personal Savior?
C. Key points on "Receiving" and "Believing"
    1. Receiving - believing; these terms are synonymous. "...many as received...even to them that believe" (John 1;12)
    2. However, the correct theological word is "faith" or "believe." Some 149 times in the New Testament salvation is based on faith as the only requirement.

THE BRIDGE OF LIFE

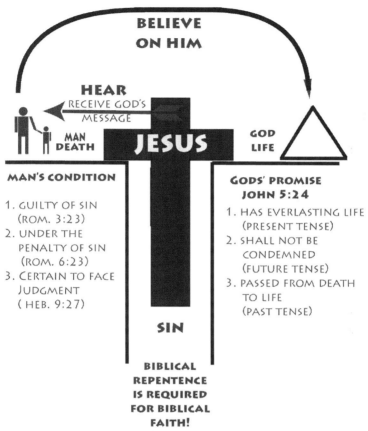

MAN'S CONDITION

1. GUILTY OF SIN
   (ROM. 3:23)
2. UNDER THE
   PENALTY OF SIN
   (ROM. 6:23)
3. CERTAIN TO FACE
   JUDGMENT
   (HEB. 9:27)

GODS' PROMISE
JOHN 5:24

1. HAS EVERLASTING LIFE
   (PRESENT TENSE)
2. SHALL NOT BE
   CONDEMNED
   (FUTURE TENSE)
3. PASSED FROM DEATH
   TO LIFE
   (PAST TENSE)

**BIBLICAL
REPENTENCE
IS REQUIRED
FOR BIBLICAL
FAITH!**

THE BRIDGES MAN BUILDS
1. GOOD WORKS
2. TURN OVER A NEW LEAF
3. EDUCATION
4. RELIGION

THE BRIDGE GOD BUILT
THE GOSPEL: 1 COR.15:3, 4
1. HE DIED FOR OUR SINS.
2. HE WAS BURIED.
3. HE ROSE FROM THE DEAD
   GIVING US VICTORY OVER SIN

3 QUESTIONS TO ASK
1. DO YOU UNDERSTAND WHAT
   WE HAVE DISCUSSED?
2. DO YOU BELIEVE GOD?
3. WILL YOU PRAY NOW TO
   RECEIVE CHRIST?

REVIEW
1. OUR SINS HAVE SEPARATED
   US FROM GOD.
2. CHRIST IS GOD'S ANSWER
   FOR SIN.
3. WHEN YOU BELIEVE,
   GOD GIVES YOU LIFE.

Chart by: W. L. Owens

NOTES

Mentor's Guide—Session 19
Personal Evangelism (II)

THE BRIDGE ILLUSTRATION

Review the assignment from session 18.

Ask about any difficulty the disciple may have incurred as he shared his personal testimony. (Stress how it is essential that ones delivery is natural. The story of God redeeming man from the penalty and power of sin must ring true from his own personal conviction. When witnessing, you must be genuine and sincere or no one will believe your witness.)

Introduce the procedure for sharing *The Bridge of Life*. Give a demonstration. Ask the disciple to study the chart and share it with someone before the next meeting.

EXPLANATION

Use a plain piece of paper and demonstrate *The Bridge illustration*. (Make the point of it being useful under almost all circumstances.)

Go over the points under section II Explanation. (The outline is rather clear and straightforward. Make sure the disciple has a conceptual understanding of the information.) Review the article: *Procedure for Sharing The Bridge of Life (page 215)*. Go over it step by step. Make certain he understands that these steps are not intended to be slavishly applied. Emphasize that he tell the story in his own words.

SUPPLEMENTAL MATERIAL & ASSIGNMENT:

Make the appropriate assignments as given on the Lesson Sheet. Make certain the disciple has a clear understanding of what is expected. Ask the disciple to pay special attention to the study of *The Bridge of Life* and be prepared to share it without notes at the next session.

Procedure for Sharing
The Bridge of Life

by Dr. William L. Owens

Conditions:

The Bridge of Life is an illustration of the Gospel and should be used in a casual setting. While it is designed for one-on-one witnessing situations, one may also use it with a large audience when employing a blackboard or projection equipment. Make the presentation private. You want a minimum of interruptions. However, the illustration can be effectively employed in a fast food restaurant. I have used it in such a setting with a moderate amount of activity.

The Process: (Follow the steps below)

1.   On a sheet of paper, <u>draw two right angles facing each other</u> as the walls of a canyon. (See *The Bridge illustration* chart. Use the chart as a reference as you follow the steps in the process.)

2.   <u>On the top of the right side of the canyon draw a triangle.</u> Label the triangle "God" while explaining that the sides of the triangle represent the members of the triune Godhead. (He alone is the only true God! He is God the Father, God the Son, and God the Holy Spirit.) Explain that God created the universe at one with Himself.

3.   On the left side of the canyon draw a stick figure and label it Man. Explain that God created man to live in blissful fellowship with Him. The condition soon changed when man chose to disobey God. Adam and Eve partook of the forbidden fruit. However, the reality of man's experience is that he is out of step with God and His created order. The sinful condition brought about by Adam's rebellion, required drastic measures which only God could correct.

4.   Vertically Print the word SIN one letter over the other between the sides of the canyon. Explain that sin is the issue that separates man from God. Define sin as rebellion against holy God or missing the mark of perfection. Man has failed to live up to his purpose for existence. Man was created to love God and to enjoy Him forever.

Sin is the problem!

5.   Under the stick figure write the word DEATH. Now list the numbers one through three as illustrated in *The Bridge* in your manual (page 211). As you list man's, condition without Christ emphasize the hopelessness of each item.
   (1.)   Man is guilty of sin—Romans 3:23.
   (2.)   Man is under the penalty of death—Romans 6:23
          Explain that this is not just physical death but also spiritual and is everlasting.
   (3.)   Man is certain to face judgment—Hebrews 9:27. Man's position without Christ is hopeless! Only an act of grace by our merciful God can meet man in his need.

6. Point to the stick figure and explain that man is inclined to be self-sufficient. He tries to solve his problem without

assistance from God. However, realizing he is not complete, man sets out to remedy his situation through self effort. For example, he may decide that he needs to educate himself, rationalizing that this would reinstate his relationship with God. Believing that knowledge is the missing link in his wholeness, man seeks to gain all the formal education possible. Upon acquiring his goal, he discovers that the fulfillment he sought was not obtained. Some may even decide that the answer to fulfillment is through religion. However, religion without Christ is a tedious matter beyond human toleration. The bridges man builds (education, religion, reformed life, good works, etc.) will never reach across the great chasm called "sin." Someone must rescue man, or he is doomed to suffer the wrath of God.

7. <u>Man cannot build a bridge to God. However, all is not lost, for God has built a bridge to man.</u> Now, draw a cross-filling the chasm between the two right angles. Explain that the cross represents Christ's blood shed in His death. God will only accept the blood sacrifice of Christ's death as sufficient payment for man's sin.

8. <u>Under the triangle write LIFE and underline it.</u> Now write in the right angle "God's Promise: John 5:24" and list the numbers 1, 2, and 3 under it as on the chart. Explain that God is the very essence of life and that He desires to share His eternal life with those who trust His Son. However, God is bound to honor His own standards of holiness and will not allow sin or those who are sinful to enter heaven. Man is in a hopeless situation unless God makes a special provision. That is exactly what God did! He provided His own Son as the ultimate sacrifice for sin. He declared

that all who would believe on Him would have the three characteristics found in John 5:24.

An easy way to remember these characteristics is to think of them as past, present and future tenses of salvation.

9. Write out the three tenses beside the numbers one, two and three.
    a. Begin by writing "Present" beside the (1) and say those who believe presently have everlasting life.
    b. Then beside the (2) write "Future" and say those who believe on Christ shall not be condemned in the future judgment.
    c. Beside the (3) write "Past," and say Man in Christ is passed from death unto life. Remind him of the need for personal repentance and faith in what Christ did on Calvary. He has promised to receive all who will believe on Him.

10. Point to the cross as you quote John 5:24.
    a. Identify Jesus as the speaker. Begin quoting the verse in phrases:
    b. Pointing to the cross say: **"Verily, verily, I say unto you,"**
    c. Shift the emphasis to the symbol for man and say: **"He that hears My word..."**
    d. Move your pointer to the symbol for God and continue to quote: **" and believeth on him who sent me, hath everlasting life,"**
    e. Point to the bottom of the chasm and say: **". . .and shall not come unto condemnation;"**
    f. Move the pointer to the word (Life) and say: **"but is past from death unto life."**

11. <u>Ask the following three questions:</u>
    a. **Do you understand what we have shared?** (Do you have any questions? Try to satisfy any lack of understanding before proceeding with the next question.)
    b. **Is there any reason why you could not ask God to have mercy on you and save you?** (This question is designed to determine the heart's desire. Make sure you do not manipulate anyone to make a false profession of faith. If you detect a serious desire, then go to the third question.)
    c. **Will you repent of your sins and ask God's Son to become your Savior and Lord over your life?** (Lead the listening soul to verbalize faith in Christ's sacrificial death for the forgiveness of sin. Help him to pray an appropriate prayer expressing repentance toward God and faith in Christ.)

Leave *The Bridge of Life* drawing in the seeker's possession for future reflection and meditation.

NOTES

222:THE MASTER'S PLAN
Session 20

PERSONAL EVANGELISM III

Assignment:
   a. Study the outline for this session.
   b. Review the *"Bridge of Life"* page 211
   c. Memorize Hebrews 9:27; 1 Corinthians 15:3, 4
   d. Study and complete the *"The Central Areas of Life Activity"* Chart - page 227

I.   Demonstration
   A. Present the *Bridge of Life* illustration: if you are in a group session make a presentation to the person next to you. If you are in a one on one mentoring process, present the Bridge Illustration to your mentor.
   B. Review verses memorized.

II. **Discussion: Salvation not by works or feelings**
God's grace + _____ = salvation (Ephesians 2:8,9; Romans 10:17)
   A. **Plus works? No!** As a means of salvation our good works are but filthy rags in the sight of a holy God (Isa.64:6).
   B. **Plus being very sorry for our sins? No!** Our sins may cause us sorrow, but that is not the basis of our salvation. Contrition or the act of being sorry is a feeling. Feelings at best are relative. What if we were not sorry enough then we couldn't be saved!

C. **Plus loving the Lord with all our heart? Again, No!**

Love is the greatest of virtues. But at the cross it is God's love, not man's that is manifested. Man simply receives it. After becoming a Christian, you should see God's love working through you to change your perspective. But, if salvation depended on man's unflinching love for God, none would attain it.

III. Presentation: Five Hinderances to Witnessing

(Review the verses listed below)

A. A lack of knowledge of God's Word will hinder your witness. (I Peter. 3:15; Psalm 119:42)

B. Negligence in prayer will hinder your witness. (You must learn to talk to God about men before you can talk to men about God.)

C. Unconfessed sin will hinder your witness. (Proverbs 28:13; Psalm 66:18)

D. The fear of man will hinder your witness. (Proverbs 29:25)

E. Procrastination will hinder your witness. (Ecclesiastes 11:4)

Mentor's Guide—Session 20
Personal Evangelism (III)

I. DEMONSTRATION
   A. Follow the instructions in the lessons.
   B. Listen for accuracy when the disciple is quoting memory verses.
   C. Make sure the verses fit the points being made in the presentation.
   D. Have the disciple repeat the presentation until his manner is natural.
      (The goal is to make the Truth in the illustration so much a part of the disciple that he can present it naturally and with conviction. His conviction must be real. He must share ownership of the message.)

II. DISCUSSION
   A. Go over the outline in some detail with the disciple.
   B. Make certain he understands that salvation is God's grace gift which we receive through faith in the sacrifice of Christ, and is not by our own works.
   C. He must also understand that Biblical faith produces a works of righteousness. (Christians do not work to become saved, but they work because they are saved.)
   D. The section on salvation and works is self-evident and needs no amplification. (Study thoroughly the subject before the weekly session. Assure yourself that the disciple understands the concepts before proceeding.)

III. PRESENTATION
- A. Go over the five hindrances to the Christian's witness.
- B. Note: Each of these points deserve your attention.
- C. Look up the Scripture at the weekly meeting and discuss how each hindrance has affected you.

SUPPLEMENTAL MATERIAL & ASSIGNMENT:

Stress the importance of making a presentation of the gospel using The Bridge illustration. Ask someone to listen to you as you share the points of truth. If no one else is available, have him ask a relative in his home for permission to make the presentation to him.

Go over the chart titled *The Central Areas Of Life Activity* (page 227). Ask your disciple to spend the next week thinking about people in each area who need Christ. Have him list their names in the applicable squares. (These will serve as potential believers with whom you may prayerfully share the gospel.)

222: THE MASTER'S PLAN
Session 21

PERSONAL EVANGELISM IV

I. **Assignment:**
    A. Review— The Bridge of Life Illustration
    B. Review— memory verses

II. **Project**
    Plan a project that will give opportunity for you to present the gospel. Choose a person whom you suspect needs Christ as Savior. Write out a practical strategy showing how you plan to present the Gospel to him.

III. **Follow-Up**
    A. Definition: Follow-up is the strategy for helping a "new" Christian become settled in the faith.

    B. Kinds of Follow-up
        1. Pastoral follow-up - I Peter 5:2,3
        2. Personal (parental analogy)
        3. As a nursing mother - I Thessalonians 2:7
        4. As a protective father - I Thessalonians 2:11

C Ways to Follow-up
        1. Prayer-I Thessalonians 3:10
        2. Personal Contact -I Thessalonians 3:10
        3. Pen—Using a letter—Paul wrote such a letter to the churches. (I Thessalonians 3:10)

4. Proxy (Send someone else in whom you have confidence.)— I Thessalonians 3:2-5

Plan to visit the person receiving Christ within one week and encourage him to guard his new faith.

This lesson completes the evangelism training section of the "222 Plan" process. The next several lessons will introduce you to different methods of independent Bible study.

Mentor's Guide— Session 21
Personal Evangelism (IV)

Some Christian workers argue that the follow-up of new believers is the most critical point in the evangelistic process. The corresponding outline for our accountability session focuses attention on the care and nurture of new confessors of faith. Follow the steps below in conveying to your disciple the basic philosophy of what Waylon Moore calls *New Testament Follow-up*. Dr. Moore wrote a book by that title. I obtained a copy for my library early in my ministry. I would commend it to all who desire to nurture new souls to the glory of God.

I. Practical Work

Have the disciple share his presentation of *The Bridge of Life*. Listen to the presentation with a discerning ear. The mentee must show a proper understanding of how Biblical faith, repentance, and the "new birth" relate. One way to pick up on your disciple's understanding of these aspects of Biblical salvation is to take note of how he uses memory verses in the presentation.

II. Project

The assigned project should be designed to create an opportunity to present *The Bridge of Life* illustration of the Gospel. Instruct the disciple to develop action steps, which when followed, will enable him to invite one to view the illustration. The setting for the presentation should be relaxed with as few distractions as possible. Instruct him to pray earnestly for God not to allow the enemy to hinder the effort.

Take note of the sample project below:

1. Pray for divine guidance.

2. Ask God to bring before you the person's name to whom He would have you bear this unique witness. (For example, let us say his name is Joe.)

3. Call Joe and invite him to have lunch with you.

4. When he accepts your invitation, offer to pick him up. Set the time.

5. At the appointed time pick up Joe and proceed to the restaurant. Select a quite place to dine.

6. Engage in conversion--set Joe at ease. Listen to him talk about things that concern him. Listen for the Holy Spirit's prompting as to when to introduce to Joe his need for God's grace through Christ.

7. If a natural opportunity does not occur, then ask if you may share the most important discovery you have ever made. (Always ask permission when sharing the good news of salvation.) If he agrees, then proceed to share.

8. Share *The Bridge of Life* illustration and ask the closing questions. If you discern grace at work in his heart, then encourage him to pray for Christ to receive him as one of His disciples.

9. If Joe invites Christ to become the Lord of his life, then offer guidance about finding a local church where he can be mentored. Offer to mentor him in "The 222 Plan."

III. Follow-Up

The outline is self-explanatory. Cover its content thoroughly. You may wish to consult other resources on follow-up. Share all you can about how critical follow-up is in the growth of the believer.

Assignments

The last sessions of the "222 Plan" process focuses on developing personal Bible study skills. Explain that rather than answer questions, we will now focus on how to do our own study. Full instructions are given for each study.

NOTES

222: THE MASTER'S PLAN
Session 22 - Bible Book Study

PERSONAL BIBLE STUDY (I)

There is no Mentor's Guide for this lesson. Follow the instructions below to complete a Bible Book Study. We suggest that you use the Book of Philemon or one of the Epistles of John. (However, 2nd and 3rd John are more difficult to outline.)

Do a basic Bible Book Study, by following the steps below:

1. Study the particular book from—
   A. A Geographic perspective.
   B. A Historical perspective.
   C. A Cultural perspective.

(The above information may be obtained from any of the good Bible handbooks available from your Christian bookstore. I would suggest *Unger's Bible Handbook*, *Erdman's Bible Handbook* or *Halley's Bible Handbook*. If you have a Bible commentary, the information you seek may be available within its pages. Another source of information may be contained in some of the "Study Bibles." If you are computer literate and are on the Internet, there are sites available to you for personal research.)

2. Read the particular book of the Bible through at least four times.

3. On the fourth reading, list the major historical events or the major topics addressed. (Historical books, such as the Gospels and Acts, should be first organized around historical events. While you may learn truths from the historical books, their purpose is not to teach but rather to tell a story. The teaching books, are for addressing issues of life and conveying information about divine principles for living.)

4. Organize your list of events in chronological order. (If you are studying a didactic or teaching book, organize your list of observations in a logical sequence.)*

5. Develop your organized list into an expressive outline of your discovery.

6. Write a summary of the book in one paragraph.

NOTE: *
Didactic means teaching. The Teaching books of the New Testament are Romans thru Jude. It is from these books that we get our instructions about how to become a Christian and how Christians should live.

An "expressive outline" is one that provides full meaning of the Scripture content while conveying the theme of the author. For an example, you may wish to consult Harold Wilmington's *Outline Bible*.

Mentor's Guide
Final Sessions 22-26
& Personal Note

Sessions 22-25

Follow the instructions for each of the individual lesson plans found in the *222 Plan Lesson* or *Session* page.

Now is the time for you to treat your disciple more as a peer instead of a follower. Our goal is to make Biblical discovery a joint effort. The various types of studies introduced are only samples of the many ways the Bible may be studied. The primary purpose for these exercises is to teach the disciple that he should learn to study the Bible for himself.

Remember one axiom: God never contradicts Himself! Therefore, look for meaning and understanding where the conclusion will honor God. Measure all your discoveries against the standard of God's Word.

Avoid being obnoxious! If you should arrive at a different conclusion from that of your disciple, be gracious. It is never good to gloat! Look for common ground in your conclusions. If there is no common ground, show the Biblical reasons for arriving at your position. If there is still no consensus, and the Scriptures support your conclusions then find a way to gently show the disciple the error of his way. One way to do this is to humbly ask your disciple to show from the Scripture the validity of his own position. Avoid being adversarial in challenging him. Let the Bible show him his error.

Session 26

You have reached the final official mentoring session. Review the overall mentoring experience and set spiritual goals for the future. At this point you may do one of two things:

1. You may terminate the process and encourage your disciple to find someone whom he may mentor in the same journey.

2. Or, you may choose to continue to meet, while your disciple mentors someone else. (In this case you are acting as consultant while going deeper by reading and discussing a book of mutual interest. Here are some examples: *Green Letters* by Miles Stanford, or *Triumph of the Crucified* by Erich Sauer.) However, you may use any book of mutual interest.

If you choose option two, then, I suggest that the reading be done at the weekly meeting. Limit the reading to one chapter each week. The reading should proceed paragraph by paragraph with each of you alternately reading aloud. At the conclusion of the chapter, each should offer a summary statement of what was taught seeking to discern whether or not you agreed with the author's presentation. If you did agree, you should provide several reasons why. Likewise if you disagree, reasons for the disagreement should be offered. Be careful that your agreements and disagreements are supported by the Word of God. The above process will increase your powers of analysis.

Personal Note

Thank you for your faithfulness to God through this learning process of investigating God's Truth. My prayer is that you and your disciple have had an experience that will change your daily walk with God and that your life will bring Him glory until He calls you home.

NOTES

222: THE MASTER'S PLAN
Session 23 - Chapter Study

PERSONAL BIBLE STUDY (II)

There is no *Mentor's Guide* for this lesson. Follow the instructions below to complete a *Chapter Bible Study*. May we suggest that you use the *Gospel of John, Chapter Fifteen*?

Develop a basic *Chapter Outline,* by following the steps below.

The *Chapter Study* is similar to the *Book Study.* The same procedures should be followed in searching out its truths. However, because of misunderstanding the differences, let us go over the steps.

1. **Pray for the leading of God's Holy Spirit in our study.**
One cannot overemphasize the importance of His participation in whatever activities we are engaged. Do not fall into the trap of making this a mechanical prayer. God is Spirit and He is a person in whose image you have been made. Therefore, make your prayer personal by sharing out of your heart how dependent you are on His revealing His Truth. Remember—your motive in seeking Truth is for the glory of God and your usefulness in His world.

2. **Read the chapter through several times.** Familiarize yourself with the content to the extent that you can share its Truth in your own words.

3. **Chronologically list the key words in the passage.** These words are usually verbs or names of issues being confronted. The chronological order is important because the Holy Spirit often reveals truth in an ordered sequence.

4. **Make a list of the truths you discern are being taught in the chapter.** Keep the truths in their chronological sequence.

5. **Organize the "truths" into a chronological outline with verse designations.**

6. **Personally apply the lessons to your own life by recording what you perceive God commands you to obey as a result of His truths.** Remember—the Word of God is not to be read or studied for the mere passing of time or for mental exercises. He has revealed His truth that you may obey Him. In obedience, you reflect the glory of His person. It is precisely here, that you will experience the *abundant life.* (John 10: 10)

222: THE MASTER'S PLAN
Session 24 - Topical Study

PERSONAL BIBLE STUDY (III)

Do an inductive study of passages dealing with a specific
Biblical topic. There is no Mentor's Guide for this lesson.
Follow the instructions below to complete a Bible Topic
Study.

1. Select a topic.
(Pray for divine leading in selecting your topic. Resist
the temptation to study a topic just to satisfy your curiosity.
Your motive must be driven by your desire to be a more
faithful servant of Christ.)

2. Select the applicable verses.
(Using your concordance, make a list of the passages that
contain your topic or subject. Be sure to honor the chronological order because revelation in Scripture is progressive.
For example, what is stated about an issue in the New Testament qualifies the Old Testament counterpart. We may
say it another way: The truths of the Old Testament are un-
folded in the New Testament.)

3. Ask the interrogative questions.
Read each passage making appropriate notations while ask-
ing the interrogative questions: Who? What? Where?
When? Which? Why? How?

4. Chronologically organize your facts.

(Review your discoveries. Look for natural divisions in the information and assign categories under which you can organize the details. List the details of your discovery under the category headings. Avoid being subjective. Do not read into the text what it does not say!)

5. Write a summary of your results.

(Include a summary statement about each of your categories including your conclusions. Relate each of the categories to the topic. Be careful to honor the teaching of the whole Bible about your chosen subject.)

6. Write a paragraph applying what you have learned to your own life.

(Ask yourself, " What does God want me to do with this information?" Don't allow the question to be rhetorical. Make yourself deal with the personal discovery of truth. God has revealed the truth for a purpose.)

222: THE MASTER'S PLAN
Session 25 - Bible Verse

PERSONAL BIBLE STUDY (IV)

Spend the next week studying a Bible verse. May we suggest that you use John 5:24. By following the steps below, you will learn the basics of doing a Bible Verse Study.

1. **Read the verse repeatedly.** Read until you have a thorough understanding of the meaning of the words and how they are used in the verse.

2. **Organize the verse into thought blocks.**
   Example: John 3:16 (King James Version)

"For God"	God	—the One who takes action
"so loved"	Love	—the motive for the action
"the world,"	World	—the object of God's action
"that he gave"	Gave	—the action
"his only begotten Son,"	Son	—the cost for the action
"that whosoever"	Whosoever	—the inclusiveness of the action
"believeth"	Believe	—the demanded response
"in him"	Him	—the object of the response
"should not perish,"	Not perish	—the escape of the response
"but have everlasting life."	Life -	—the promise of the response

2. **Develop your captions into an expressive outline of your discovery.**

Example: GOD'S SALVATION (John 3:16)

I.   The Innovator of Salvation—God
II. The Motive for Salvation—Love
III. The Object of Salvation—World
IV. The Act of Salvation—Giving
V.   The Cost of Salvation—God's Son
VI. The Inclusiveness of Salvation—Whosoever
VII. The Condition of Salvation—Believe in God's Son
VIII. The Person of Salvation—The Son of God
IX. The Negative of Salvation—Shall not perish
X.   The Positive of Salvation—Everlasting Life

3. Write a summary of the verse in one paragraph.

Example:
God is the initiator of salvation. It must all begin with Him. He loved His creation so much that He is not willing that His creation should perish because of sin. God offers His Son's sacrifice to be effective for all who will believe (trust and rely) on Him. Such belief will result in being pardoned from Hell and given everlasting life. To perish is to experience the second death and spend eternity without God forever. To have everlasting life is to have Heaven and experience God and His love forever.

Epilogue

I hope that your experience as a mentor has exceeded your expectations and has created in you a desire to seek another with whom to make "the journey." The one factor that I did not anticipate when I began my journey in mentoring, was the profound level of bonding and commitment I witnessed. In all my teaching experience, I have not seen the development of this level of love and respect for a teacher or pupil. The mentor and mentee relationship is unique to this teaching process.

Over the decades, I can remember the ones who have taken the journey with me like Frank, Lance, Tom, Randy, Bill, Randall, Ron, Fred, and Ernie. The churches I have served are also special to me, because they were the Lord's assignment for the church and for me at that particular time in our development. I have come to understand that God not only develops individuals for His glory but also congregations. Congregations and pastors are fitted together by the Lord directly related to His will, His purpose, and their needs.

I think, that I now understand why the Lord had Paul write Timothy about teaching others what he had learned through mentoring. Blessings are immeasurable when this unique process is used as an instrument of instruction. A mentor not only shares the Truth of God, but he shares himself. That is something Jesus did with Paul; it's what Paul did with Timothy; it's what Timothy did with faithful men, and that's what faithful men did with others.

We continue it today as the mandate of Christ. Fred shares with Tom, and Tom shares with Bob. On it goes, as disciples of Christ are developed and bonds of love are fashioned in a brotherhood like no other.

We encourage you to visit the 222 Plan website where you can catch up on the latest news and disciple-making information. Type in the following address in your Web browser: WWW.222plan.org. Until next time, happy mentoring.